# How To Replace Congress©

I0409313

## WITH NON-PARTISAN & CONSTITUTIONALLY RECOMMENDED TERM LIMITS

# HOWARD HANSON

# Dedication

**For those who love living in the Republic
Of the greatest country in the world,
The United States of America**

*"If there can't be peace between two people, how can there ever be Peace in this World?"*

*-- Howard Hanson*

*"The hope of a secure and livable world lies with disciplined nonconformists, who are dedicated to justice, peace, and brotherhood. The trailblazers in human, academic, scientific, and religious freedom have always been nonconformists. In any cause that concerns the progress of mankind, put your faith in the nonconformist!"*

*-- Martin Luther King, Jr.*

**HOW TO REPLACE CONGRESS ©**
**With Non-Partisan and Constitutionally**
**Recommended Term-Limits**

Copyright © 2016 by Howard Hanson. All rights reserved. Except for quotations in reviews articles, no portion of this book is to be reproduced in any manner without prior written permission from the publisher. www.HowToReplaceCongress.com Email the author at howard@howtoreplacecongress.com

# Acknowledgements

To the Republican and Democratic parties; for their inability to get along with each other, and for their desire to keep incumbents in office for unlimited terms. To our Forefathers, that had the wisdom to have term limits in the Constitution. To my Father for the long hours of conversation on our political system.

*"Term limits have always been in the Constitution."*

*~ Howard Hanson*

# Table of Contents

# Prologue

## Why Did Senator Term Limits Happen by Class?

Many people have been interested to learn that term limits for U.S. Senators are spelled out in the Constitution. Not by Amendment, but in Article I from the time it was written. The Constitution even elaborates why the text was fashioned this way. For some reason, we just weren't taught this important knowledge in school. Maybe it was a nation-wide "fail," but the fact is that we weren't taught term limits in school. The idea of term limits for Senators and Representatives didn't come up in American History class, Civics class, and not even in any of our college courses. In fact, while interviewing teachers, professors, and even a federal judge – no one had heard of this wonderful idea.

Term limits are a simple and an effective way to replace Congress without losing the affectivity of government. What a novel idea! On top of that, we can get rid of the old belief that anyone with enough money can buy Senate seats year after year. The option for that financially blessed individual or PAC to keep a partial proponent in office would go away entirely. Our legislators will have you believe that re-election is a natural and legal aspect of holding political office. Yet the Constitution never mentions the possibility for any Congressperson to be re-elected after their term has run out.

The beauty of this concept is that it has been there all along, for 229 plus years. It has simply never been brought to our attention. Hmm! Maybe the fault is with our education, or perhaps something else is influencing the information that we receive. In fact, it wasn't until 1940, that only 50% of young adults even managed to go to school long enough to earn a high school diploma[1] It wasn't until "Constitution Day" on

September 17, 2004, that a federal law was passed which required all federally funded schools to provide a course on the Constitution. The law only set the minimum requirement for one day in one class and the duration of one hour. One has to wonder whether the students receive a Democratic or Republican version of the class, depending on their teacher. It truly is amazing when people think that their party is the right party. It doesn't matter; it's Congress. The government is a single unit made up of three classes, all of which are entirely replaceable.

The fact that Americans still don't know that term limits are in the Constitution is a puzzle. When I bring it up in conversation the first thing I hear is, "Have they made an Amendment to change term limits?" The answer is no. From a political standpoint, the party system wouldn't want us to know this fact, even if they did have a knowledge of it themselves. This is just something that has never been addressed or implemented, although you can find each public official's termination on the senate.gov site.

Can you imagine the problems that would have been eliminated or reduced without all the past and existing political corruption? All the staging of wars and military conflicts, setbacks from bad economic decisions, corporate collusion, conspiracies, and the trillions of wasted tax dollars, along with the loss of American jobs to name a few? When you look at all of Congress, many current congressmen have been in office longer than Obama, George W. Bush, Clinton, and George H.W. Bush combined. **Have we seen any reduction in government with that seasoned bunch of legislators?** Some have even been in office since Ronald Reagan, Jimmy Carter, Gerald Ford, Richard Nixon and Lyndon Johnson. Listing all the military actions enforced by Congress in that time frame is another book in itself. In the last 50 years, the Presidents have changed, but the **Congresses** have been very much the same.

10

On a positive note, term limits might have a significant impact on how we wage wars and take military action. , If one-third of Congress were replaced every two years we would be limiting the legislative body's ability to enter into conflict with other countries unless we were attacked. Putting together enough power and incumbent backing within two years in order to wage war would surely be difficult because in the next two years two-thirds of Congress would be replaced. Intercity issues come to mind as well; if all aldermen, councilmen, state legislators, mayors, and all agency supervisors had term limits – corruption would be curtailed to some degree. We wouldn't have 4 of the seven last Illinois Governors in prison. That is only the beginning of a long list of politicians in prison.[2] Consider the many real-life examples we have seen short-tenured leaders – such as in the case of a massive company bringing in a new CEO only for a couple of years to turn the company around. The extent of this awakening is truly endless, and so are the changes it could bring when term limits happen by class.

*"Redundancy is the foundation of education, redundancy of having the same Congress is a disaster."*

*- Howard Hanson*

*"Whether you think you can, or you think you can't--you're right."*

*- Henry Ford*

# Introduction

*"Those who cannot change their minds cannot change anything."*

*- George Bernard Shaw*

It only takes 90 seconds to share this interesting narrative about Congress. Once you learn that our government officials have term limits, you may be overwhelmed with another burning question; "Why does the greatest government in the world keep this astounding treasure of information hidden from its people?"

Indeed, the US Congress has grappled with divided support for quite some time. Loyalty to particular parties divides us while widespread nationalism unites us – but of course, that depends on your age and other demographics. Freedom of speech may be one of our golden rights, yet we often hear the phrase, "If you don't like America, nobody is stopping you from leaving!" Freedom has been a hot button issue since the inception of our great country. We live with the gripping fear that our Constitutional freedoms will be torn away from us at any moment. With some of the worst rated Congresses in the last couple of decades, perhaps the fear of losing our freedom is not surprising. At a July 14, 2013, interview on NBC's "Meet The Press" regarding reforming Congress, Senator Harry Reid stated bluntly:

*"Is there anyone out there in the world, real world, that believe that what's going on in the Congress of the United States is good? Our approval rating is lower than North Korea's."*

*How To Replace Congress* is not about disliking America or thinking there is a better government in this world. What's important is to realize how people of all ages seem to be **conditioned to set aside common**

**sense and reasoning** when it comes to the morality of our Congress. With the exception of some true policy experts and the more astute folks working on Capitol Hill, any conversation about Congress seems to send its participants into a zombie-like state. Influences from the media have served to exacerbate the confusion by misdiagnosing the problem as a symptom of party failure. The result is a widespread belief that if one party could just take complete control of Congress and the Presidency, all of our problems will be resolved. This book will illustrate just how misguided such thought systems are by revealing the very secret that our government has kept from us for far too long.

The wait is over, and the secret is out. **According to the Constitution, one-third of Congress should be voted out of office every two years.**

*How To Replace Congress* brings this and other secrets to light, and lays out concrete steps towards turning our government around and truly making this country great again.

America's history is woven with examples of how its citizens have moved to change and improve government. It all began with the original colonies that were fed up with how they were being governed and decided to compile a list of their complaints and declare their independence from the oppressive influence of Great Britain. Their unhappiness with the government echoes the same issues that we have today; the violation of our natural laws of human rights, our privacy, our liberty and the pursuit of happiness - all are either being controlled or taken away by our government. At times, the methods of control are not so obvious, but the consequences are overwhelming. We see evidence of this in the government's exclusive possession or control of scientific knowledge designed to advance a better way of life. How many of us voted to explicitly allow the government to read our emails or tap into our phone conversations? Why has the government created massive security agencies through the pretended offenses of terrorism? If these actions are truly being carried out for the greater good, then let the people speak on these points by voting in an open, honest system. It's time to take a stand and demand that our government abides by the Constitution. We must stand up for our rights and reclaim our freedom by creating a voting revolution.

Our nation was designed to be run by the people and not by a political party, special interest groups, big money, or people who have defied the rules to stay in Congress for longer than six years. The party system may not allow us to elect a president that truly represents what the people want, but we can still choose to have one-third of Congress replaced every two years if we are willing to step outside the party system to look for candidates. This book is going to reveal concrete steps towards electing an entirely new government in the course of six years.

My discovery was more of an accident while researching what could be done peacefully about our political system so that we would have more control over who is in charge and how we are being governed. This was more of an awakening, as the answer has been right in front of us for over 240 years. The truth, like most things, always hides in plain sight. In this case, it was right on the first page of **Our Constitution,** a document that expounds on the **"federal law of how the government would operate."**

The Constitution is currently being violated by the legislature established for the voting system. Voters cannot enforce the Constitution because they have not been aware of its true contents. The Constitutional laws designed by our forefathers shows us how to vote and why to vote that way. It's this discovery that needs to be shared in detail not only with all Americans but also with other nations around the world.

*"It's quite obvious that we will never know to ask the second question unless we are aware that there is a first question. Now we have discovered the first question."*

*- Howard Hanson*

**First question:** Did you know our Senators were set up in classes?

33 - Class I,  33 - Class II,  and  34 - Class III Senators  =  100 Senators (two per State and no State has two senators form the same class).

**Second question:** Why did the Constitution dictate that we should separate our senators into three classes?

**So that one-third of the Senate would be replaced every two years:**

> 34 – Class III Senate seats Expire     November 2016.
>
> 33 – Class I    Senate seats Expire     November 2018.
>
> 33 – Class II   Senate seats Expire     November 2020.
>
> 34 - Class III   Senate seats Expire     November 2022.

Non-Partisan was the goal of this book. I did not choose which party that an individual belongs to that may be in this book. Their name may be mentioned because of a position they hold or the length of time they have been in office, or that they were involved in some legislation that is mentioned in this book. So, I am asking kindly before you make any judgment about a comment being partisan please read the entire book to get the true message of what I am trying to communicate.

# Chapter One

## It's on the First Page of the Constitution

*How To Replace Congress* was written to help voters regain control over elections and ultimately have better leadership.

The stark realization that the key to our entire system of government is on the very first page of the Constitution is dumbfounding. Article I clearly states that "the House of Representatives shall be composed of Members chosen every second Year by the People of the several States." The same notion is thereafter supported in part six of the article, demonstrating how the Senate shall be constructed. "[T]hey shall be divided as equally as may be into three Classes. The Seats of the Senators of the first Class shall be vacated at the Expiration of the second Year, of the second Class at the Expiration of the fourth Year, and of the third Class at the Expiration of the sixth Year, so that one-third may be chosen every second Year."[3] Notice that there is no mention of the word "re-election" in this text. In fact, the current government has verbally added this convenient phrase to their slogans in order to create the illusion that re-election is normal and to be expected.

In simple terms and black and white letters, our forefathers explained that Congress is interchangeable and is not created to have permanent posts. "We the People" had the clarity and foresight to determine these rules and lay them out first, above all else, in the Constitution of the United States. Our founders felt that these regulations were necessary to avoid tyranny and totalitarianism. They carefully crafted each section of this concise document to give our country the best chance at maintaining fair and free elections and equal representation across the board. At what point in our 240-year history did we lose sight of our freedom of choice?

16

The truth has been buried so deeply below the tired rhetoric of incumbent politicians, that voters have abandoned the polls almost entirely. In 2014, the Census Bureau found that just 41% of registered voters showed up to exercise their freedom of choice in the Congressional elections.[4]

As a result, we have given that freedom of choice to a government body that does not represent our best interests. The power we have given these misrepresentatives has been wielded disproportionally to control our economy, impose unfair regulations, restrict freedom of speech, inhibit free trade, and implement mass government surveillance over our private lives. These impositions should sound familiar, particularly since the horrific tragedy that afflicted America on September 11, 2001. This tragedy and countless others should never have happened. Perhaps we can prevent similar tragedies from happening again, but we must act quickly and determinately. We need voters to use reasoning and common sense in 2016, 2018, 2020, 2022 November elections. By following one simple rule, we can change the course of history, and steer America back to safety and prosperity. This book contains a clear guide that will help voters understand whom not to vote for in the coming Congressional elections. It's time for us to get back to our roots and demand that our Congress abide by the Constitutional law of "Six Years & Out of Politics."

# Chapter Two

## Let's Start With The Good News

The good news is that "Six Years & Out of Politics" does not require us to partake in the age-old party rivalry that has divided our country for decades and continues to instill separatism in our united nation. Whether voters are Republican or Democrat doesn't matter. The party system as a whole lies at the core of keeping incumbents in office. *The Constitution of the United States does not begin with the words, "We The Parties," nor does it state that we should divide ourselves along party lines. So we either vote patriotically as a Republic by stepping outside of our two-party system, or we continue down the faulty path of party-line loyalism. I am not suggesting a further decentralization into liberal, centrist, conservative or Tea Party voting, but rather the use of the clear directive given by the authors of our Constitution.*

*"If there can't be peace between two people, how can there ever be peace in this world?"*

*-- Howard Hanson*

Many consider themselves experts on the matter of American politics. They claim to understand the insider lingos and agendas and speak confidently on the on goings and opinions of other Congressmen although they are not elected officials. Let me be clear; every word these "experts" say can be nothing more than hypothesis and speculation. Congress operates behind closed doors – that means restricted access and secrecy. Even opposing parties do not have access to the true proceedings taking place behind the closed doors of their adversaries. It's my sincere hope that this reality, along with many others, will set in as you read this text.

18

If you're still reading, thank you. I hope that it means that you are interested in changing our Congress and spreading the message to your fellow voters. I am impartial to your party affiliation. My desire is to introduce you to one of the most important sections of the Constitution and to help you spread the truth that will help us regain our freedom of choice.

Changing Congress will also make for a stronger Presidency. This can be done in at least three ways:

1) The House of Representatives has the sole Power of Impeachment. By regularly electing new representatives, we can be more effective in checking our Presidents' executive orders;

2) Elected public servants will be encouraged to work together in making good decisions for America; and

3) We will diminish and hopefully abolish the influence of Political Action Committees, on how Congress legislates.

Another intention of the book is to give voters a greater understanding of how legislators are *selected by the party system* rather than *elected by the people*. You will discover how each political party compels us to vote for their selected incumbents. Incumbent members of Congress have impressive records in getting re-elected, with roughly nine out of ten winning their re-election.[4] We need to overcome this unfair advantage and create a level playing field for new candidates.

> *"Sometimes in life, it's as important to know what we shouldn't do, as it is to know what we should do!"*
> Howard Hanson

Voting should not be a dreaded chore and a crisis of decision between the lesser evil. We should feel good about voting, and have confidence that we are making the right decision.

With a clear directive, we can have an immensely positive impact on our country's politics as well as its future. Together, we can re-build Congress, have a real choice of Presidential candidates, and begin to re-build America.

Upon completion of their six years, senators shall vacate office, step down and let new people, new talent, and new ideas flow into the system of government.

The Constitution says, "The Seats of the Senators of the first Class shall be vacated at the Expiration of the second Year [....]" The words, *"shall be vacated"* do not imply "get re-elected," or "go to another office," but to leave office entirely. This means you must pack your stuff under the watch of security and be escorted out of the building. How do you interpret the words "shall not steal," or "shall not kill"? Do you agree that "shall vacate" doesn't mean *maybe*, doesn't mean *possibly*, doesn't mean *probably*, it means you *will* leave?

The Federalist Papers, written by Alexander Hamilton, James Madison, and John Jay, and published in 1787 contained 85 articles and essays that urged for the ratification of the Constitution. The authors supported the original wording of the Constitution that prevents re-election of the same politicians, stating that "[t]he qualifications of the persons who may choose or be chosen... are defined and fixed in the Constitution, and are unalterable by the legislature."[5]

In fact, our Constitution quite clearly states the exact limit of the senatorial term. You can find the text in the 17th Amendment of Article 1, Section 3: "The Senate of the United States shall be composed of two Senators from each State, elected by the people thereof, for six years, and each Senator shall have one vote."[6]

You may already have burning comments or opinions regarding what you've just read.

However, please have an open mind to the possibility that this book is a call to action and one that is better than most alternatives.

How do we accomplish the task of weeding out career politicians from our government? The answer is simple. We do this by using the list of individuals who have been in office for a minimum of six years to vote out those incumbents that have completed their Constitutional term. It's a simple, no-nonsense way of approaching what *not* to do when we go to vote.

It's our responsibility as the governed of this country and the determinants of its future to educate us about the candidates who are vying for office. Nonetheless, political research is a truly tedious undertaking. The honest truth is that we're just human – not all of us have the time or tools to take on such a responsibility. So ask yourself, can't there be a simple way to vote without doubting yourself every time you're facing the ballot?

The answer is yes. Like flipping the switch to light a darkened room, we can flip the switch and stop voting for politicians who have been in office for six years or longer. Want to simply things even more? Don't vote for incumbents and don't vote for politicians.

An ex-politician or a politician going from one office to another is not a public servant. How many more mayors, governors, legislators, aldermen and even judges need to have allegations of wrongdoing before this hard truth sinks in? History shows that the longer some politicians are in office, the more opportunities they have to break the law or abuse their position. Illinois has had particularly bad luck with their recent officials. Four out of the last seven governors are currently serving out their sentences in federal prison.[7]

This book is designed to help lead all of us towards making better decisions when it's time to vote.

It was written to show us that we have **term limits**. The shocking reality is we've never used them. It will help uncover why we vote the way we do and what we can do to make a change. The remedy is simple – requires only one step: vote out incumbents and unprincipled politicians.

*"A just estimate of that love of power and proneness to abuse it which predominates in the human heart is sufficient to satisfy us of the truth of this position."*

*-- George Washington*

# Chapter Three

## 1789's Early Warning Signs About Political Parties

In his Presidential farewell speech, George Washington warned us of the danger that lurks around over-dependence on any political party. He urged people to place their identity as Americans above their identities as members of a state, city, or region and focus their efforts and affection on the United States above all other local interests. Washington further asked people to **look beyond political parties** and argued that **every government** has recognized political parties as an enemy and has sought to repress them because of their tendency to seek more power than other groups and to take revenge on political opponents. The following are a few selected quotes from pages 14 – 19 of Washington's farewell speech where he warns the United States citizens about the drawbacks of a party system and career politicians.

*"The name of American, which belongs to you in your national capacity, must always exalt the just pride of patriotism more than any appellation derived from local discriminations.... Here every portion of our country finds the most commanding motives for carefully guarding and preserving the Union of the whole.... In this sense, it is, that your Union ought to be considered as a main prop of your liberty and that the love of the one ought to endear to you the preservation of the other.... One of the expedients of party to acquire influence within particular districts is to misrepresent the opinions and aims of other districts.... You cannot shield yourselves too much against the jealousies and heart burnings which spring from these misrepresentations."* [6]

*-- George Washington*

**Over 150 years later, we received another somber warning, but once again we did not listen.**

Dwight Eisenhower is one of many presidents that has warned us, *"Our hard work, resources, and livelihood are all involved; so is the very structure of our society. In the councils of government, we must guard against the acquisition of unwarranted influence, whether sought or unsought, by the military-industrial complex. The potential for the disastrous rise of misplaced power exists and will persist. We must never let the weight of this combination endanger our liberties or democratic processes. We should take nothing for granted. Only an alert and knowledgeable citizenry can compel the proper meshing of the huge industrial and military machinery of defense with our peaceful methods and goals so that security and liberty may prosper together."*[8]

*--Dwight Eisenhower*

When our founding fathers penned America's Declaration of Independence from Great Britain's oppressive rule, they made it clear in our Constitution that the American system of government was to be a Republic. The Declaration was designed as a blueprint to help guide our nation's government into a peaceful democracy. Our early leaders emphasized the power of the people to replace elected representatives frequently so as to avoid falling back under the rule of a single ruler, monarchy or family. Nevertheless, we have allowed the party system to speak for us for over 200 years. They have done us wrong, and it is time that we stand up for our Constitutional rights and put in place a new Congress.

## Let's review the two phrases in the Constitution that will put this all into context:

**Article I Section III Says –** "The Senate of the United States shall be composed of two Senators from each State, chosen by the Legislature thereof **for six Years**; and each Senator shall have one Vote."

The next paragraph states, "The Seats of the Senators of the first Class shall be vacated at the Expiration of the second Year, of the second Class at the Expiration of the fourth Year, and of the third Class at the Expiration of the sixth Year, so that one-third may be chosen every second Year;"

It is clear from this succinct description of the government structure that it was left up to the people to use their vote to dictate political leadership. Once each Senator reached a maximum of six years of service, they must be **vacated** from office.

**Under Term Limits -** The six-year Senate term represented a compromise between those framers of the Constitution who wanted a strong, independent Senate and those who feared the possible tyranny of an aristocratic upper house, insulated from popular opinion. **Under Senate Classes -** Constitutional commentator Joseph Story (1779-1845) explained the reasoning behind the Senate's class system.

"Framers hoped biennial elections would bring stability to the Senate, and in turn, to other branches of the new government. By gradually changing members, class rotations would prevent senators from permanently combining for "sinister purposes," protect the Senate from a rapid turnover in ideas, and encourage senators to deliberate measures over time. Most important, as the

25

federal government's only continuing body, the Senate could provide leadership after major elections and during other periods of national uncertainty."[8]

**Article I Section II Says** – "The House of Representatives shall be composed of Members chosen every second Year by the People..."

These are the peoples' term limits. *How To Replace Congress* is urging voters to remind career politicians that they are breaking the law by staying in office for longer than six years. A voting revolution is the only way to overcome the current party system. [9]

# Chapter Four

## Can We Just Stop Hating Each Other For Four Days?

Decisively, the fact that any single Congressman's reputation has become tainted even a little should be cause enough for alarm. The daunting reality is that many of our politicians have criminal records or are headed for lengthy prison sentences based on corruption charges during office. This fact should give us reason enough to clean house and start over. It won't be hard to find public servants to replace the politicians. It may be more difficult to find voters who will be willing to let go of voting along party lines.

In today's ever more connected world, we sometimes find it difficult to make time for things that require our attention. As a result, we rely on sound bites and quick spurts of information to stay up to date on current events and relevant information. Politicians have capitalized on our newfound attention deficit disorder and shortened their campaigns to repetitive sound bites that don't even begin to explain their true platform completely. It is, therefore, imperative that we as voters **use Sense and Reason** when it comes to electing officials to our government.

**Reason:** For over one hundred documented years, our elected representatives have failed to police themselves. Wrongdoings both great and small are often swept under the rug and forgotten. The magnitude of this effort tends to be wildly the opposite when the opposite party is trying to get elected. During election time, each side pulls out every piece of dirt they can to destroy their opposition. *How To Replace Congress* suggests that we take incumbents out of the equation and bring in new public servants to serve us.

Democrats hate Republicans, and Conservatives hate Liberals…okay, we get it. But what happens if we just stop hating each other for four days? **Sense:** These days don't even have to be consecutive, they just need to be the next four days that we vote for the future of our country: *Day 1 - November 8, 2016; Day 2 - November 6, 2018, and Day 3 -November 3, 2020*, and Day 4 – November 8, 2022. **Reason:** If we lay our differences aside, and trade emotional matters for rational truths – we can implement, "Six Years and Out." This would allow America the opportunity to take in fresh talent, knowledge, and energy.

Our armed forces risk their lives every day, fighting for our security and freedom. We can thank them by upholding the Constitution at home. Let's unite to raise the American flag and stop hating each other for just three days!

## All That Wasted Money!

Yes, there will be a lot of Political Action Committee (PAC) money wasted trying to keep this broken voting system from changing. There are a handful of entities that will spend upwards of $430 million dollars just for the 2016 elections for House and Senate incumbents. This money is used to buy your votes in order to keep current politicians in office. **Reason:** Don't take their bait! Not voting for incumbents is equivalent to enforcing term limits. **Sense:** No matter how glamorous their campaign promises sound, incumbents will not get it done. **Reason:** it will take an entirely new Congress to keep **any** promises heard on the campaign trail, not just an individual. **Sense:** it's time for us to remind Congress how long their positions are designed to last.

In 2000, the Supreme Court held that blanket primary voting violates a political party's freedom of association under the First Amendment.

**Sense:** Why, shouldn't we be able to vote for either party in the primaries? What the Supreme Court said is that the party can give you just their ballot without including the names of opposing party candidates. **Reason:** This is a political action and not a public action; once again the party is doing us wrong. Even the Federal Judges are appointed by "legislators" for life – a fact that will not change until we have new legislation.

## Even The Chief Justice Doesn't Care How Much Money Is Wasted On Campaigning.

On April 3, 2014, Chief Justice John G. Roberts Jr. took campaign finance to another level with this written comment, *"Government regulation, may not target the general gratitude a candidate may feel toward those who support him or his allies, or the political access such support may afford."*[10]

**Reason:** if our government can't or won't create regulation to stop legislators from showing their gratitude to super PACs, who will? **Sense:** The answer is "we the people." By exercising term limits, we ensure that incumbents cannot be re-elected and therefore would have no use for PAC money

What's "a little"? PAC's spend billions of dollars keeping legislators in office, and they want ten times that amount in return. It's alleged that Comcast alone spends around 18 million dollars for elections. That's not much considering that their annual revenue stacks up at over 60 BILLION. FYI, technology companies along with most PACs, make sure that both parties are covered with campaign donations. PACs, don't care which party is in office.

It's just a tiny down payment that has a HUGE return on their campaign investment.

**Reason:** When funded by PAC money, incumbents know that the support doesn't come for free. They must return the favor, as per the words of Chief Justice John Roberts Jr. Favors go to interested organizations in the form of support for specific legislation. It seems doubly ironic from this perspective that incumbents do not find it necessary to show their gratitude to the voters, being that their campaign has probably used matching federal funds at the cost of taxpayers' hard earned dollars. **Sense**: Wouldn't a lawyer call this a conflict of interest? Hint: The answer is a resounding "Yes." Having learned all this, who's best interests do you think are being spelled out in our legislature? Does it seem fair that our taxes go towards the salaries of hundreds of government officials that don't act on our behalf? Who is the government working for at any rate?

**Reason:** The simple law of action and consequence can be called on to determine whether special interest plays a role in policymaking. Thomas Edsall, a writer for the New York Times once mused,

> *These are extraordinary times. The depth and strength of voters' conviction that their opponents are determined to destroy their way of life has rarely been matched, perhaps only by the mood of the South in the years leading up to the Civil War.*[11]

Voters are further enraged when they discover that lobbyists and special interest groups are perpetuating the corrupt practices of government but skirting laws and finding loopholes in regulations. Edsall writes,

> *In practice... the lobbying industry is moving below the radar. More than $3 billion is still spent annually, more of which is not being publicly disclosed. Corporate America is relying on new tactics to shape the legislative outcomes it wants.*

*In fact, lobbying techniques have evolved so as to elude the regulations that implement the 1995 Lobbying Disclosure Act. These regulations are revised every 6 months in "written guidance on LDA registration and reporting requirements" issued by the Clerk of the House and The Secretary of the Senate.* [12]

Most of the thousands of lobbyists work across the city, in and around K Street. In the past decade, a news source reports that 18 lobbying firms, corporations, and labor unions have purchased town houses or leased office space near the Capitol. Lobbyists have found legal ways to skirt around contribution restrictions by wining and dining their favorite Congressmen at their own homes, giving them time to rub elbows and shoptalk. The catering bill is written off as a contribution to the lawmaker's campaign. [13]

**[Sense:]** It's not very smart of us to continue allowing legislators and PACs to be in that position, is it? This is just a small window into how incumbent campaigning has hidden cost to taxpayers. We pay their salary for six years of working, and yet they still spend a good amount of time in their first and last year campaigning.

## Total Congressional Salary is Over $1,044,000.00 For Each Period of Six Years.

A gigantic salary is one more example of why it doesn't make **sense** to allow consecutive terms. **Common sense** would dictate that if someone is not doing their job, then they should not get paid. Most people don't know that each member of Congress makes about $174,000 a year whether they are working or campaigning. That amounts to $1,044,000.00 in return for their alleged service to the people.

Keeping conversation as non-partisan as possible is the most effective way to instill the term limits outlined in the Constitution. The goal is not to be a one-sided freedom fighter or the beginning of any revolution; it is about being objective to real-life issues. Talking about politics is pretty simple when one uses facts and a non-partisan approach. We could take into consideration that most voters identify themselves as Centrist, which in turn underlines that these voters don't care which party is in control of the House or Senate. Our hope is that this impartiality will lead centrist voters to one of two conclusions: they will take the list of whom not to vote for when they cast their ballot, or look at the list of current incumbents from their State and do their research before entering the voting booth.

# Chapter Five

## We Didn't Vote For The Individual We Voted For The Party

We want choices, but we are currently limited to mostly incumbents because of the two-party system that distorts our voting process by only allowing us to vote on a one-sided ballot. That's not what it means to have the freedom to vote or the freedom of choice. For over 150 years, we have held on to the false hope that the incumbents chosen by the party will do a better job in the next six years. History has shown us that it doesn't matter which party has control of Congress because money from various Political Action Committees (PAC) helped get them elected and kept them in office. The PACs have destroyed the American Dream!

The only responsible way to vote for an incumbent or a repeat politician is by following these prerequisites first:

1) Research the individual and their affiliate party to see how they have voted in Congress. (Who has the time for that?)

2) Examine the committees that the incumbent is part of to determine whether a conflict exists. Example - Do they oversee any industry that has donated to their Campaign? Most likely, the answer will be, "Yes" because the incumbent votes as part of Congress. A conflict of interest is unavoidable.

3) Check on which bills they introduced or co-authored to verify whether that the bill is in the best interest of the people or the best interest of the PACs. (No time for this either, but at least we can assume that the PAC interest wins over our own).

4) Investigate if they were part of a larger group of legislators that could not or would not attempt to have a federal budget (We know that they exist, yet we do not consider the budget when it's time to vote).

5)     Have they rescinded any laws that have impacted our
Human Rights?

If we don't do the research, are we guilty of voting for the party instead of the individual? It is the party that brings incumbents to our broken Congressional voting system, and they don't care. They are in it for control of Congress.

The word "legislation" is closely interchangeable with "political party." You may agree when you hear or read statements like, "One party chose to agree with the XYZ Law of 2016 and the other party voted against it." The division and indecisiveness within Congress are fueled by PAC money that influences how your politicians vote for the legislation. To block incumbents from basing their legislation on such misguided decisions, we must replace one-third of Congress every two years.

Career politicians lurk outside of Capitol Hill as well, and can be found in your very town, city, and state. For the politically career minded, the gubernatorial post is a good place to start. If any governor has been in the same office for four years or longer – it's probably time for a change. This is especially true if they have come from some other government office to get that position. Choosing to serve in public office for longer than six years is often a move towards making politics a career. **Sense:** When are we going to realize that this is a loss to society and not vote for them?

Many readers are familiar with the politicians Ronald Reagan and Rick Perry. Both incumbents switched parties. Perry's political career is an example of how an incumbent attempts to move up the proverbial Congressional ladder, even if it takes crossing party lines. District 64 elected Rick Perry to the Texas House of Representatives as a Democrat in 1984. Most of us also know that he switched parties to be a Republican so that he could become Lieutenant Governor under George W. Bush.

34

He subsequently joined the Tea Party to run for president. **Reason:** The point is, do we care about any individual's party affiliation? One of Rick's famous punch lines is, "Let the voters decide!" Well, let's just use, "Six Years & Out," as our voters' punch line to decide whom to vote for. Reagan's comment was, "I didn't leave the Democratic Party; the party left me." **Sense:** Let's use our vote so that one-third of Congress is replaced every two years. **Reason:** We can go back to voting for a specific party when we start to see a difference, but we need to treat Congress as an entity, so we have a new government every six years. Wisconsin's governor Scott Walker is another example of a career politician. He's never held a private sector job, yet he has remained a Republican all his life. The important part of this story is that you don't need to have legal or private sector experience to be a politician; what you need is someone or something like the Koch Brothers backing you with an estimated eight million dollars! They are also the alleged owners of a not for profit organization in Wisconsin called Focus on Energy. Consider whether these facts make logical sense. Let's review:

**Sense;** This is a prime example of how not voting for incumbents would keep outside money out of politics. Plus, what does it actually take to be a "politician"? **Reason:** Who would give someone eight million dollars if they couldn't be elected again?

Haven't you asked why they funded him in the first place? Hmm, was it because they aren't from Wisconsin but have some vested interest in legislation that affects the Badgers state? The people would like to hear that argument's line of reasoning.

**Reason:** think about this; the party system doesn't give us any choice of whom to vote for other than incumbents. In turn, we as voters close our eyes as we cast our vote for someone that has been promoted to govern us by receiving massive amounts of PAC money without our ability to questioning the reasons why!

In some cases, when we do get a chance to vote for more than one person in Congress, we can only vote for the party and not for any other candidates! This is just another voting law made to keep legislators in office. We may not like voting for the opposite party, but we can only hope that we learn that doing the same thing for over 228 years is rendering results that aren't working.

**Sense:** the consequences of not acting quickly and decisively to change how we wield one of our most impactful rights of freedom – our vote -- can, and likely will be of catastrophic proportions. It is already evident to both Democrats and Republicans, and all opinions in between, that this country is on a rolling rampage towards trouble. This self-evident truth has people thinking and talking about its future in a way that is downright unnerving. The word "revolution" echoes on the lips of many people with too much casual ease. A worrying example has been exhibited in the Donald Trump rallies. Are we allowing domestic terrorism to occur in the name of patriotism by failing to condemn these violent protests? Or, is Trump possibly a candidate that is willing to communicate what most Americans believe and want for our country?

Trump's unique non-party platform* includes bullet points like safety from those who are threatening America, better border protection, bringing jobs back to America, stabilize our financial system and "Making America Great Again". **Reason:** Isn't this what our Congress should have been doing all along?

One of the main reasons I felt compelled to write this book was for fear of a true non-voting revolution. I have heard too many people utter the words that it will take an armed revolution to change our government. It is that phrase that I can neither accept nor ignore. It was that statement that allowed me to overcome my fear of your reading my less than stellar grammar to get this message out. So, please get past the grammar and read into the real message. Thank You!

\* **Non-party platform explained** – a person that could have been a candidate for either party. Eisenhower was an example as he was supported by both parties however, he was elected president as a Republican. Mr. Trump could have run as a democrat or independent. The point being we need to be thinking about non-politicians and staying non-partisan. What we need to be thinking about is only voting for public servants. As you read through this book you will find that many of you may have voted for an individual that switched parties just so they could run for that office.

# Chapter Six

## How Can We Fix Our Current Voting System?

We start with finding the different ways we can get more people to vote. The book is designed to give us confidence when it's time to vote and confidence to talk to others regarding how they feel about Congress.

**Electing** one-third of our Congress happens every two years.

**Reality:** It will probably take one generation (20 years) after we start the voting process to replace all of Congress!

Insofar, our attempts to remedy stalemates and lame duck Congresses have been a complete failure. For America, it's been over 200 years of misrepresentation and abuse of power. New, smaller parties have cropped over the years, including the much-publicized Tea Party – a branch of the Republican Party Creating new parties does not address the real problem, only a symptom of the political illness at hand. **Sense:** the real problem has been the consistent lack of opponents – a problem that will persist until we begin to replace one-third of Congress every two years. We have had 114 opportunities to rectify this issue. This coming November 2016 will be opportunity number 115. This will make Congress 230 years old, so is it time for us to make the proper changes? We do have a choice; we can either leave Congress alone or bring in 334 new members [see list in the back of the book] that have served over six years. Some people are calling to replace all 469 that are up for election. Unfortunately, you are also going to see how the US government has created diversions under the guise of First Amendment violations that hinder large groups from peacefully gathering to talk about politicians.

It is common knowledge that once an incumbent has settled into office it's difficult to tell which party they belong to, that is until we see their voting record. It will mostly be party line voting.

38

We don't need more parties or larger Super PACs; we just need to follow the Constitution, and help Congress vacate office.

This step-by-step plan indicates how we as citizens can peacefully move our country towards positive change by voting independently for a common cause. If applied, this voting system will ensure constant turnover of any elected public official. It could also be used to rid us of bureaucrats that have controlled agencies for over six years. Leaving a post does not imply that the incumbent should then move to another federal or state agency but rather be barred from any taxpayer-funded post, indefinitely. It's time for federal public workers and bureaucrats to go back into the private sector. Having them out of government would help to eliminate possible subversive activities that would influence government officials and negatively impacts citizens.

## The Impact of Our Votes

*"Never doubt that a small group of thoughtful, committed citizens can change the world. Indeed, it is the only thing that ever has."*

-- *Margaret Mead*

Examining the life and work of Lyndon Johnson will show us how powerful someone can become by being in public office for too long. Johnson's actions continue to hinder voting today. Lyndon had a real fear of voting power when he was in office. He tried to squash his fear by taking away the First Amendment rights from churches in 1954.

*"The vote is the most powerful instrument ever devised by man for breaking down injustice and destroying the terrible walls which imprison men because they are different from other men." - Lyndon B. Johnson-*

Once our votes are placed, they impact us for at least a half a decade. In many cases, your voting decision may impact this country for twenty to forty years.

I know forty years may sound ridiculous, but the list of individuals who have been in Congress for too long continues to grow. Here's a short-list of reasons why our votes currently impact us for such an extended period of time: the two-party system and their incumbents run Congress, fulfilling the wishes of the rather than the people; the complex mix of propaganda spawned by lobbyists, and our politically charged media keeps pushing us to vote for the same officials in office; those officials don't get along with the opposite party once in office; therefore they can't make decisions.

We have heard excuses time and time again from one party or the other claiming that they can fix all our problem if they could only have control of both chambers of Congress, or the presidency, or all three! They also fight tooth and nail to have their preferred candidates appointed for life as Supreme Court Justices – a revered yet supposedly non-partisan post!

## Long-Term Politicians Make All The Final Decisions Whether A Law Is Constitutional Or Not

Both political parties are aware that being aligned with their side isn't the same as being aligned with the people's rights or desires. I am hoping this description makes it clear how a politician is a loyalist, not a patriot because of the flaw in our voting system. Legislators from both parties have passed laws whether they are Constitutional or not.

What is worse, it is nearly always the case that the most dictatorial and bullish of these lifetime politicians also transition into leadership positions that speak for the entire group – such as Minority or Majority House or Senate leader. Doesn't unilateral control by one party sound more like an authoritarian form of government? Both parties are guilty of becoming belligerent towards each other; and when they're in control, arrogant, domineering and almost dictatorial.

This kind of power and control could not exist if one-third of Congress were replaced every two years. There is still time for a change, and the opportunity to replace one-third of Congress happens every even-numbered year.

## The Chicken, Or The Egg?
I am not saying the stock market and elections are connected.

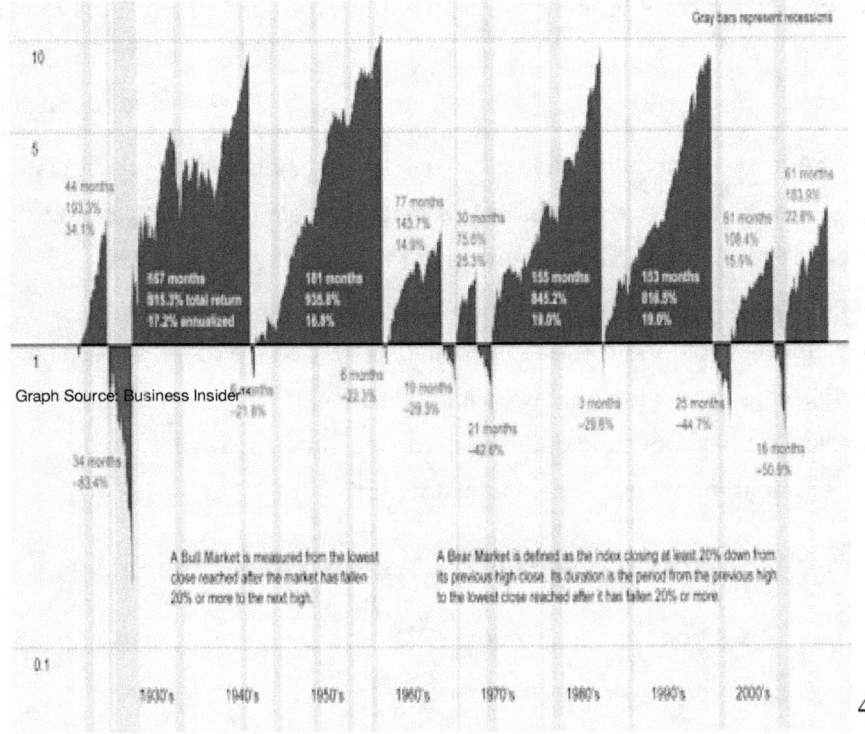

Graph Source: Business Insider[14]

41

However, there have been a few bear market distractions on several even numbered years. Here are some notable bear stock markets in even-numbered years; 1930, 1938, 1946, 1962, 1976, 1982, 1990, 1992, 1998, 2002, 2008, 2010, (defined by a 20 percent drop in the stock market) and what is going to happen in 2016?

In 2014, in the voting game for the Senate race, the Senate Democrats warned Obama. They were concerned that any bold executive action ran the risk of upending the chances of several Democratic incumbents running for re-election in the southern states where Obama is unpopular, and the issue of immigration reform isn't as urgent. What happened? Republicans won the seats to take control of the Senate and the House.

We all know that voting out one-third of the Senate is essentially an impossible task. But with a little humor, we have to remember that impossible tasks just take a little longer to achieve.

*"I'm a great believer in luck, and I find the harder I work, the more I have of it."*

*-- Thomas Jefferson*

Achievement of the impossible can be done in a few simple steps. First, we need to have the desire to change something. Once we start the process of eliminating incumbents and replacing them with public servants, a greater number of high-quality candidates will become available in each party. The term "politician" will cease to have meaning, as this career-oriented post will simply disappear. We can still have political parties, but candidates won't be incumbents. We will have a government run by public servants, not parties or PACs.

## Money Will Still Try To Buy Our Votes.

The billions of dollars super PACs spend on incumbents is to get our votes in return for the incumbent Senator or Representative to vote in their favor. As you can see, all that PACs have to do is keep incumbents in office, and they get what they want. If incumbents can't be re-elected, the power of the super PACs to control elected officials is abruptly snatched away.

When considering the persistent problem of career politicians, we must also take into account major federal agencies like the United States Departments of Labor, Education, Agriculture, Energy, Health, and dozens of others. These governmental bodies could also benefit from change. For instance, instead of having a career position as the head of an agency, the creation of an elected Board of Directors may serve the people in far more democratically. The directors, much like congressmen, would be limited to two or four years in office. However, we may not see any agency changes until we change one-third of Congress every two years. Imagine the difference we can make if every four years there is a new majority in Congress!

## A New Challenger Threatens An Old Tradition

In 2016, Donald Trump is running as a non-incumbent non-politician and is in the forefront over both the Democrat and Republican parties for being the next President. One of Trump's incumbent opponents, Ted Cruz put up a ver table fight with major help from PAC money in late January of 2016. An alleged superfund PAC created by a few billionaires (some rumored to be involved with oil fracturing) have donated tens of millions of dollars to his campaign. Why? Congress and the Supreme Court may not see anything wrong with this scenario, but perhaps that is because they are all recipients of PAC money in some shape or form, so why would they? Of ccurse, it's wrong! In the face of this level of corruption, we are left with only one choice: stop voting for incumbents.

A Harvard study found that in the last decade, only 22% of incumbents in the U.S. House of Representatives had any significant challenge to their seat in the primary.[15] It's no wonder that they don't worry about our votes. In another recent Harvard study, they reported that "the probability that an incumbent in the United States House of Representatives is re-elected has risen dramatically over the last half-century; it now stands at more than 98%."[16] So their real survival to keep power depends on convincing us that we can't vote them out. But we are not helpless in the face of these statistics and odds. We now know that by using the Constitution, "The Federal Law," we can vote incumbents out of office.

## The Power of the Silent Majority

A democracy allows us to be organized in a way that can make our votes extremely effective. Take a moment to think about how truly powerful our vote can be when it's used to be socially impactful. These are a few ways our vote can be more useful: 1) We have the power to create and exercise term limits; 2) We start to clean up how our State governments are run; 3) We elect officials that are representing the people; 4) We shut down money flowing to corrupt politicians as campaign contributions won't make sense. That is if we follow Article I using the every two-year rule and having one-third of Congress booted to make room for fresh faces and perspectives. Follow these steps and you will create a voting revolution.

**Sense:** to test this concept on voting, ask your friends, coworkers, and family some of the following questions:

"Do you think we should have term limits?"

"Would you like to have better choices of who we get to vote for?"

Then ask, "Do you think the two parties should work together in Congress instead of constantly working against each other?"

**Reason:** if they say that this will never happen, you will know that this is an opportunity worth sharing. You can help awaken our Silent Majority, which may be up to 60% of all people that can vote but don't. All it takes is asking a couple of questions.

Those of us that say that these necessary changes can never happen usually agree that the changes are necessary, but don't know how it may be possible to make the dreams a reality. They understand, just like you and I that getting the Congress that is truly elected by the people is going to be a challenging endeavor. However, if you get a "yes" to any of those questions – and the likelihood is that you will -- you can share how one-third of Congress could be voted out every two years. We have needed something written about *How To Replace Congress* for a long time. From the very birth of our country, we have had a great need for a document that specifies how we should vote to maintain a healthy democracy and avoid corruption in government.

Now, with the help of this book, we have a document that can give us concrete steps that are easy and simple to implement. We know we have always had a right to vote, however voting with the power to make a difference wasn't taught to us in school, in our community, or at home. Most of us have followed the social status quo, which aligns us with one party or the other. After reading this book, hopefully, we can work together to change that. When we vote in the future, we will have the confidence in making good voting decisions!

Other countries will possibly follow America's lead if we change how we vote. Having spoken with different customer service reps from around the world, I've found that they have the same problems with officials being in public office for too long. This problem exists in every country.

The problems identified with selected leadership are magnified with time. This fact should be common knowledge, but it is difficult for us to believe that this level of corruption is happening under our noses, right here in our great country of America. Once someone is elected, they know they have at least an 80% to 90% advantage over anyone else trying to get elected[17]. The same can be said about our American Royalty, as you will see discussed in later chapters. Another truth we must try to remember as we cast our vote is that during election years, there is some entity donating huge amounts of money to keep an incumbent in office. Unfortunately, these selected officials will do whatever they can to keep their job.

As a Harvard study points out,

*"When they become term-limited...the option of staying put is no longer available and, thus, the costs of running for the state's upper house decrease substantially. In these circumstances, we expect a higher number of high-quality candidates to decide to challenge the incumbents than we would have otherwise."*[17]

Hoping an incumbent is going to change or make a difference is like buying lottery tickets and "hoping" that you win mega millions. The probability is 175 million to 1. We have better odds of looking at our history of failed Congresses. We should quickly realize that keeping them in office because of experience is a worse option than making a change.

The odds are against voters when an incumbent is trying to stay in office. Parties and legislators have found ways to write laws that give them extreme advantages. We, on the other hand, have the federal law of the Constitution on our side. The recent comments of Mitt Romney and others in the Republican Party may help in waking the sleeping giant, our Silent Majority.

They are showing us that they believe legislation has developed a sense of elitism. The history of Greek democracies shows that their biggest fear was that the common people could vote out the elite. Legislators are not the elite; they should be working for America and its citizens. They have certainly shown us their true colors. In return, let's show them our vote.

# Chapter Seven

## Enforcing Federal Law on Government Operations

The sworn oath that was taken by elected officials for "public office" has nothing to do with swearing an oath to a particular party or pledging loyalty to that party. It's required that all legislators swear an oath to uphold the Constitution, which is the **Federal Law on how the United States Government is to operate and an oath to be loyal to the people**.

Reviewing the Constitution's preamble says volumes regarding the foundation and very nature of public office in the US, and the fundamental principles that this country was built upon. The Constitution is the Federal Law of how our government is to be run. They are basic laws of who, what, why and how they will protect the rights of the people. Legislation has minimum rights in the Constitution - rights that are assigned to them by the people. For the government to write more laws that give them more power is wrong. They have overstepped the boundaries of the Constitution and have done so because they write the laws that say it's OK to do so.

## No One Knows How Many Federal Laws Exist!

I will suggest more than once that there should be a website with a list of Federal Laws. One important list that we should create and check often is that of the Federal Laws currently active that violate our Human Rights. People should know these laws and have the opportunity to vote on whether or not they are Constitutional.

Yes, I understand this will take time to create. However, go to the government sponsored sites, and you will find that they don't know the number of Federal Laws! This is not being functional, practical or realistic, yet our Congress has allowed this to happen. This is what one government site has to say; "*however, a total count of laws passed does not account for the fact that some laws are completely new; some are passed to amend existing laws, and others completely repeal old laws. Moreover, this set does not include any case law or regulatory provisions that have the force of law.*"[18]

The fact that our government doesn't even know how many laws we have is one more example that we need to have an electronic library that can keep meticulous and automatic track of our legal system. The Internet wasn't built overnight, and I guess that we would have plenty of open source entrepreneurs willing to help put this list together. This book is about building a solid case that the word broken doesn't even begin to describe our Congress. Words like inoperative, malfunctioning, disrepair, failed, unsettled, troubled and dishonored are a few that would help describe our current state of government. After having won an election, each senator must be sworn into office as per our Constitution.

**Mandated Oath by Article VI; its text is set by statute (5 U.S.C. 3331).**

*I do solemnly swear (or affirm) that I will support and defend the Constitution of the United States against all enemies, foreign and domestic; that I will bear true faith and allegiance to the same; that I take this obligation freely, without any mental reservation or purpose of evasion; and that I will well and faithfully discharge the duties of the office on which I am about to enter. So help me God.*[19]

It is easy to see that for the last several decades or longer, our elected officials have let this country down in their sworn oath.

The introduction of the Constitution is called the Preamble. It begins with the words, "We the People…", and is followed by the Articles that clearly demonstrate what our government stands for. Each senator and representative of the Legislative Branch of our government swore an oath to uphold these Articles and has failed miserably in upholding that oath. We are ashamed of our legislators, and they should be ashamed of themselves. What makes our predicament even more frightening is that **they don't even seem to care**.

## The Constitution of the United States

### The Preamble

*We the People of the United States, in Order to form a more **perfect Union**, **establish Justice**, insure **domestic Tranquility**, provide for the **common defense**, promote the **general Welfare**, and secure the **Blessings of Liberty** to ourselves and our **Posterity**, do ordain and establish this Constitution for the United States of America.*[20]

## How are Republicans and Democrats Upholding the Preamble?

Before we begin, please take a moment before jumping to some pre-determined conclusion about the following comments. Get ready for a shocking fact. The United States budget is never reviewed in detail by anyone - not even Congress. This analogy is like saying the Model T was the best car ever made.

Or pick some other car - it doesn't matter. The point is, cars continue to be improved upon to provide a better experience to the consumer, and also reduce waste and harm as bi-products. Continuous improvement is achieved by bringing in new people and new ideas to build upon the basis of what is already there.

We need to set aside any initial judgment regarding budgets or the concept that our government could not possibly be improved upon. I want to specifically ask that we momentarily dismiss the dogmatic patriotic mantras like, "America is the best country in the world," and "America's political system and government are flawless and better than any other." I'd like for you to keep all of that passion for your country while staying current on the newest available information and technology. Now, let's get on with needed critical improvements.

We are living in a depressed or false economy. Only a new Congress can put the necessary actions into motion that will begin to cure this ailing economy effectively. History shows us that budget cuts are only part of the solution. Reducing tax rates will promote a spending economy. When we have extra money in our pockets, we feel that we can spend more on eating out at restaurants, entertainment, travel, and even that fancy cup of coffee. When we want to spend more money on leisure activities, we increase demand for these goods and services, and the businesses that provide them can grow and expand. With business growth naturally comes job creation. Solutions such as this one are already on the table – why is Congress not willing to bring us renewed hope and prosperity by applying these simple concepts?

The inability to act but one of many failures that we encounter with our current egislature.

Taking into account just the preamble of the Constitution we can determine where Congress has upheld its oath to the people, and where it has failed the country miserably.

**"Form a more perfect Union" – [rating - failure]** Federal Government continues to disturb several states bordering Mexico. This seems to be a real issue when it comes to illegal immigration. The result creates considerable conflict with Texas, Arizona, California, Florida, Louisiana, New Mexico and New York. Heath Care is also being left to the discretion of each State. A recent study by the Society of Actuaries found that "there will be significant variation across states in the impact of the Affordable Health Care Act (ACA) on average cost"[21] for individuals and families purchasing healthcare coverage on their own. State and local governments are currently drowning in a sea of Federal red tape and regulations.

It's virtually impossible to make long-term financial business decisions when a bureaucrat can develop yet another regulatory restriction in Washington at any given time. The Health Insurance Portability and Accountability Act (HIPAA) has been one such law that has affected many people and their relationship with health care negatively. It's a law that some may say has gone too far or amiss.

The main tenets of HIPPA are as follows;

- Provides the ability to transfer and continue health insurance coverage for millions of American workers and their families when they change or lose their jobs;
- Reduces health care fraud and abuse;
- Mandates industry-wide standards for health care information on electronic billing and other processes; and
- Requires the protection and confidential handling of protected health information

The confidentiality required by HIPAA is one aspect of this law that may be applied in ways that are inappropriate. Anyone caregiving for a loved one could tell you many of the undesired ramifications of HIPAA. I had the misfortune of experiencing these ramifications one day when my car failed in a hospital parking lot. The hospital claimed they could not look up the license plate of the car blocking it, as they claimed the employee was protected by HIPAA. Seven hours later the car owner (a doctor who parked in a visitor-only parking space) moved for the day. Does anyone see anything wrong with that subsection of HIPAA?

As another example, HIPAA protects those that are diagnosed with mental illness, giving them the right to have a fair background check. It's important to understand and support our Second Amendment as it was put into place to protect our Bill of Rights. However, if someone was diagnosed and confirmed severely mentally ill, shouldn't the FBI be allowed to include that information in a background check?

"There's wide agreement among 90 percent of Americans that we need to keep guns out of the hands of people suffering from severe mental illness," says Colin Goddard, a survivor of the Virginia Tech shooting who is now the Senior Policy Advocate for the Everytown for Gun Safety movement.

Following the release of an alarming report called *Fatal Gaps: How Missing Records in the Federal Background Check System Put Guns in the Hands of Killers*, many states were moved to improve their standards for record reporting. The article had a measurable impact as reporting increased three-fold. Sixty-five percent more individuals whose record indicated a dangerous mental illness were prevented from purchasing guns at the store.[22]

This anecdote is a great example of how such preventative measures can actually reinforce our Second Amendment by emphasizing that gun ownership can be practiced safely.

When it comes to forming a more perfect union, our elected legislation needs to keep the party system from having control over ballot creation and designation of district lines. The case in the point is, the current primary ballot makes it mandatory to designate a party preference for you to be able to vote. It should be designed to give the power of candidate nomination to the voters. Voting along party lines takes away our Constitutional right with regards to whom we want to elect to be our leaders. Our Constitution is not set up to allow the party system to rig votes in order to be able to keep as many of their incumbents in office as possible.

**"Establish Justice" – [rating -failure]** There are too many federal agencies that employ authorized personnel to make arrests. These are just a few federal agencies that may need to be un-super-sized.

## How Many Agencies Do We Need?

The NSA, CIA, TSA, FBI, DEA, ATF, DHS, IRS, CBP, FEMA also the U.S Marshall. Do you think each branch may be a bit out of control and seemingly run by bureaucrats that head the agency? It's Congress that oversees them. Many of these agencies implement violations that are infringing on our rights. The Declaration of Independence called them usurpations, defined as taking someone's power or property illegally or by force. [20] So where is the Agency that supports our Constitution and protects our rights as Americans? We have never voted to allow our government to encroach upon our personal rights and freedoms, yet it has been doing just that since 1791.

# The Un-Patriotic Act

It's our Bill of Rights that is always under attack by these agencies, and our selected legislators are not defending them. Many agencies hide under the Patriotic Act that really should be called an Un-Patriotic Act. Why? Because they are in our homes, our cars, and everywhere else, we seem to be. What is patriotic about monitoring our phones, our exact location at any given time, recording all of our emails, every website site we have "ever" looked at, and all of our purchases and other activities? As far as we know, they are keeping those recordings indefinitely. See the PBS episode of "Nova: Rise of the Drones"[23] for more of what we have to look forward to.

Other government agencies like the FDA, USDA, DOE, EPA, and Department of Health and Human Services, are responsible for the oversight, regulation, and establishment of US policy. This means that they regulate how Americans can or can't do almost anything in the United States. There is an astonishing amount of over-regulation provided by the US Food and Drug Administration [FDA] on food products, pharmaceutical, medical technology, medical process and nutrition. Who is overseeing this unjust and outdated legislation? The answer is, "no one." The reason is that we are too busy or too stressed out to make the effort. Many feel that they have been taught not to talk about politics or religion. This concept sounds like social propaganda.

**Amendment 1** – *Congress shall make no law respecting an establishment of religion, or prohibiting the free exercise thereof; or abridging the freedom of speech, or of the press; or the right of the people peaceably to assemble, and petition the Government for a redress of grievances.*

Legislation impacts all individuals on many levels - from executives, management, doctors, lawyers, scientists, and accountants to educators, farmers, small and large businesses - all of us. A book called "Outsmart Your Cancer" shows at least ten cures for cancer that had been developed over the last 100 years and used by the medical society until each method was mysteriously rejected from practiced medicine. Agency laws are injustices that violate our First, Third, and Fourth Amendments ceaselessly.

**First Amendment– Prohibiting The Exercise Of Free Speech (**see statute 501 3c): A federal law that prohibits tax-exempt organizations from endorsing or opposing political candidates or the publishing or distributing of statements in any political campaign. This brings to mind the McCain-Feingold Act, a federal law that in essence outlaws and prohibits corporations and unions from criticizing incumbent politicians 60 days before an election. Failure to comply can result in penalties of up to $250,000 and loss of exemption for violating. Feingold & McCain are running again. FYI, John McCain is a Class III Senator and according to the Constitution shall vacate office upon the expiration of his class. "All" 34 Class III Senate seats expire in November of 2016. Feingold is trying to get back into the Senate. However, he was first elected in 1992 served 18 years and is looking for another six years! Maybe he will make a campaign promise to rescind that bill as it certainly could impact him (a non-incumbent) from getting elected. This is the irony of life.

**Third Amendment - No Soldier Shall, In Time Of Peace Be Quartered In Any House, Without The Consent of The Owner, Nor In Time Of War, But In A Manner To Be Prescribed By Law:** They are in our house, if; we have a phone, a smart phone, the Internet or even cable TV, constantly listening and recording every word that is said. They also do this under the guise of the Patriotic Act.

Comcast is also in your house if you use their service. Comcast corporate can turn your remote control on or off. When called on it, all they say is that they have the ability to reset your remote control! What else are these companies doing? You know that tiny camera that is on your cell phone? Do a search on hidden micro-cameras and microphones in your TV. They have been in our computers for over ten years it was just a matter of time before they made it into our TVs. I recently spoke to a young sales rep at a national electronics store. When I asked him what he thought about the camera phenomenon, he said we demanded it because we want instant customer service! There was a time when things made in the United States actually worked and we had great customer service. Can the user shut off this "customer service" feature of the camera? If not, it is an invasion of privacy. Having micro-cameras and microphones in TVs is a little more than interactive! Be advised: wear a long shirt! Oh, by the way, unless you unplug your TV, it's still on.

**Fourth Amendment– The Right Of The People To Be Secure In Their Persons, Houses, Papers, And Effects, Against Unreasonable Searches And Seizures, Shall Not Be Violated:** This amendment is violated virtually every moment of our daily lives, and a good example is once again the Internet. The government sees and stores all the information easily found about almost everyone on the world wide web, including your date of birth, your home address, phone number, place of work, what your home looks like, and many times what vehicle you are driving, among many other things. Oh, and don't forget to see if your TV or set-top box has those special features you weren't aware of but apparently demanded.

**Fourteenth Amendment - Citizenship Rights, Ratified 7/9/1868.**

The Fourteenth Amendment allows anyone born in the United States to be a citizen. This amendment has been a real problem with illegal immigration even before WWII. Remember, this law was written in 1868 and from 1892 to 1954 immigrants came in through Ellis Island. Now they land in one of the 30 plus international airports, shipping lines, or of course walk or fly across any of our borders illegally. Being a natural born citizen allows you specific rights, including the right to vote, freedom to stand for public office and invest in U.S. real estate. Are they truly standing for America?

They may want to rethink this one. For instance, a woman affiliated with a terrorist organization has a baby in the U.S. After that, she immediately goes back to her home country and raises her child as a terrorist until the age of 16. That child comes to America, completes college, and at age 25 can be a Representative of the House. Five years later, at age 30 he can rise to a Senatorial seat or even campaign for Presidency of the United States! Sound like fiction? The reality is stranger than fiction. Ask Ted Cruz.

**Posterity - [rating -failure]** This is defined by our future generations. The US Government has created a horrifying future for you and I, for our baby boomers, and for each generation thereafter. We currently hold a debt so large that our children's children may not be able to pay off that enormous amount of money. Some estimates say it is around $50,000 for every person living in the United States. Congress may have done a good job in securing welfare for themselves but not for future generations.

## Injustices, Corruption & Failures

See below how these types of injustices violate our 1791 First, Third, and Fourth Amendments at all times. Why don't our legislators bring this to our attention and maybe ask for some constructive ways we could help?

**Common Defense - [rating -failure]** The government has failed to adequately protect our borders. This would also include reviewing outdated or un-enforced immigration laws like the P.L. 94-571 Adjustment Act of 1966, which expands on the Cuban Adjustment Act of 1966, allowing Cubans to automatically become American Citizens after one year of residency – regardless of how they came to this country.

## Twelve-Plus Agencies and We Still Have an Immigration Problem!

It has been suggested that the annual illegal immigration rate in the U.S. is approximately one million people per year, with an estimated 11.7 million illegal immigrants in the U.S. at this time.[24] It stands to reason why one of the strongest points of our Constitution was to protect our borders. All three branches of government should be ashamed of themselves and us as voters for keeping the incumbents that don't enforce border protection in legislation. This is not a question of *how* can our borders be protected but rather a question of *when* we can achieve this necessary protection. Currently, a decision won't be possible on an even-numbered election year. Hoover, Truman, and Eisenhower all had to deal with deporting millions of illegals from the United States.

Here's an example gleaned from www.businessweek.com - "In 2014, with their control of the Senate in the balance,

Democrats had pressed Obama to delay action on immigration, arguing the issue would work against reelection of several incumbents facing strong Republican challengers."[25] Then again in 2015, immigration and protecting our borders are at the top of the list for the presidential debates. This will go on throughout 2016 and possibly 2017 without any resolution by Congress, just false promises or false hope of what can or could be done.

**Domestic Tranquility - [rating -failure]** Our country is facing a profound imbalance in many areas of domestic life: an overwhelming number of homeless citizens, home foreclosures, high health-care cost, high energy cost, irrationally high costs of communication and internet, and heightened rates of unemployment.

They claim there is little to no inflation in the U.S.; haven't they ever bought gas, paid electric utilities, paid heat bills, went grocery shopping, paid the ever increasing unregulated cost to watch TV, internet, or have a phone? Let's not forget property taxes. You can buy a 55" Smart TV for under $500, but you still pay at least that much for a smartphone! The word "Sheeple" comes to mind. All of these costs continue to increase our everyday expenses, and yet the government claims that there is little to no inflation. A performance based Congressional and Presidential salary is only a dream at this point, but it would cause them to take action if it could be implemented.

**General Welfare - [rating -failure]** This refers to the common good and should be beneficial for all members of society. When I say all members, I mean all - from the one-percenters to the homeless and everyone in between. Illegal immigration is out of control. Consequently, our education system, healthcare, and the United States infrastructure all need to be brought to the top of the decision-makers' agenda. The United States may have the best government - yet changing the way we vote would make it even better.

**Blessings of Liberty - [rating -failure]** Our freedoms are being challenged daily by government agencies with their intervention into our lives. Our liberties were quickly taken away under the guise of domestic terrorism. We should use our Constitutional liberty to vote, and reinforce the idea of a people's Democracy in this country.

As President Obama put it in a speech addressing the United Nations, "*...nations that have persevered on a democratic path, have emerged more prosperous, more peaceful, and more invested in upholding our common security and our common humanity.*" The President was talking about how the people's vote makes a difference. "*Time and again, nations and people have shown our capacity to change - - to live up to humanity's highest ideals, to choose our better history,*" he continues, "*That is why we look to the future not with fear, but with hope.*"[26]

Any legislator currently in office who has sworn to uphold the Constitution has not done so. To uphold the Constitution, a government official would have to protect our rights and be willing to blow the whistle on him or herself and their colleagues.

**Article I Section 6 has this to say;** *They shall in all Cases, except Treason, Felony, and Breach of the Peace, be privileged from Arrest during their Attendance at the Session of their respective Houses, and in going to and returning from the same; and for any Speech or Debate in either House, they shall not be questioned in any other Place.*

**However, Article II Section 4 – Disqualification** Says something a little different; *The President, Vice President and all civil Officers of the United States, [Congress] shall be removed from Office on Impeachment for, and Conviction of, Treason, Bribery, or other high Crimes and Misdemeanors.* Bribery can be defined as informal palm greasing; also shouldn't a misdemeanor be defined as showing favoritism while in session or for allowing special deals from PACs?

## Definitions Also Neglected In The Constitution:

**Shall** – expressing an instruction or command, expressing the future intention [Listed in Article I Section 3 Claus 2]

**Vacate** – leave give up (a position of office), (a place that one previously occupied) [Listed in Article I Section 3 Claus 2]

**Shall be Vacated at Expiration** – A command or instruction to leave in a fixed period of time. [Listed in Article I Section 3 Claus 2]

**Expiration** – the ending of the fixed period for which a contract is valid

**Misdemeanor** – misconduct; mismanagement, neglect of duties, improper behavior [Listed in Article II Section 4 – Disqualification]

**Redundancy** – one-third of Congress can be replaced without a loss of their function, the state of no longer being employed

The above could all be considered grounds for impeachment of Senators, House Representatives, Judiciaries or the President. This is not to suggest that we start an impeachment process. It is one more example as to how efficient and effective our votes could be.

*"I believe we possess all the resources and talents necessary. But the facts of the matter are that we have never made the national decisions or marshaled the national resources required for such leadership."*

*- John F. Kennedy*

# Chapter Eight

## Why Replace One Third Of The Senate Every Two Years?

Currently, we are not controlling our voting system - it's been controlling and compelling us. The fact that we have electors for our electoral college is a sad joke. Do you know anyone who is an elector in your state or any other state? Didn't think so, most people don't, as they are controlled by legislators and not by voters. Legislators are in turn controlled by their respective parties, and the parties that control the primaries. It's also the party that picks who we get to vote for. The primaries and the caucuses are set up by the party system and designed for that specific party. The opposite party isn't even there.

Whew, that was exhausting just typing it! The fact is, we are socially trained how to act and what to believe in depending on which party we align ourselves with. Ask yourself this question, "Which party do I align myself with?" If you said neither party, I'm a centrist or progressive, great answer. Now let's vote like we mean it. That is the thought that should be going through American's mind when election year comes up.

There is a lingering question regarding who precisely is controlling the political parties and thereby controlling the rest of this country? We don't know who "they" are, but have no doubt that they are controlling you too. We just don't want to think of it that way, so we continue to vote the way we have in the past.

**"Six Years & Out"** - The beautiful thing about "Six Years and Out," is that it was planned at the very inception of our country's government. The following is put into context and taken from Article I, Section III, Clause II of the Constitution.

## The Law That Never Was

*"The Seats of the Senators of the first Class shall be vacated at the Expiration of the second Year, of the second Class at the Expiration of the fourth Year, and of the third Class at the Expiration of the sixth Year, so that one-third may be chosen every second Year."* **This federal law that is contained in the Constitution can only be upheld by the people.** We have entrusted Congress with our livelihoods, but there was never an agreement to take away our freedoms. Congress has been infringing on our liberty for at least 100 years. This is one of the most powerful arguments supporting the idea of replacing one-third of the Senate every two years. The same concept should be applied to rejuvenating the House Representatives.

## Why We Don't Know About The Phrases, "Shall Be Vacated," or "At The Expiration Of Their Class."

Having interviewed dozens of eligible voters, not one person knew that Senators belonged to three different classes. This is one of the reasons why you read the words, *shall vacate* so frequently in this book. Ask everyone you know if they can answer the following three questions!

**Ask Three Questions:**

1) Did you know that Senators were in classes?

2) Do you know why the Constitution assigned them into classes?

3) Do you know why we have a new Congress every two years?

The classes were designed so that one-third of the Senate would be replaced every two years. It was set up that way so only one senator from each state would be replaced at a time. Additionally, we were to have a new Congress every two years with one-third of that Congress consisting of new people.

## A Lot Can Happen In Six Years

How many times have you heard someone say that we need to get rid of everyone in Congress? That we need to throw all of them out and start over? Frustration gets people to say many things, sometimes without thinking it through. We all know those thoughts happen all too often and for millions of people.

The wise architects of the United States Constitution anticipated what could happen in the duration of six years, and they were right. They already knew the frustration that comes with an inadequate legislative body. Term limits were created with these truths in mind.

*How To Replace Congress* advocates these standard term limits - two years for House Representatives, six years for Senators and four years for the President. Some might argue that the public office terms are not long enough. I present a counter argument and ask, "What do they need that much time for?"

My friend Joe commented that if we were to abide by term limits, the bureaucrats would know that their boss would be in office for only six years. Joe argued that this would create a bureaucratically controlled government.

If this is truly your concern, then name a legislator that you have personally voted for who got rid of any bureaucrat or reduced the size of any single agency. Can't think of any? Imagine that.

Remember it's only one-third of Congress that would be replaced every two years, so their bosses will not be affected by the spring-cleaning. There is no single individual overseeing the bureaucrats, but rather Congress as a whole plays the collective boss role. Bringing in a new boss is always an uneasy feeling for bureaucrats.

Under a new Congress, bureaucrats should be more concerned with their roles in the government because they will ultimately be pushed to represent what the people truly want. The Declaration of Independence was written to avoid infringement on our rights and freedoms as human beings. These fundamentals are entirely lost to us if we side with the PACs and career politicians who are only looking after their distinct interests.

## What Can Be Accomplished In Six Years Or Less?

Some people think six years is not long enough so here are a few thoughts of what can be done in a very short amount of time:

The Empire State Building was built in less than two years.
The Hoover Dam was built in less than six years.
The Pentagon was built in 16 months.

During World War II, the United States built over 200,000 planes, over 50,000 tanks, and over 2,000 submarines – all in just six years. All were shipped on over 3,200 ships - built in those same six years.

Take a moment and think of what can be done in six years and the amount of planning and infrastructure that needed to be built or put into place in those six years. We will never forget what Germany, Japan, Great Britain, Russia and dozens of countries accomplished in those six years. Far be it for us to forget the millions of lives lost in the same six years. It becomes glaringly obvious that six years is more than long enough. In many cases, it's too long to keep the same legislators in office and feed their hunger for more power.

# Chapter Nine

## The Mighty Midterm Elections

I myself really never knew how important midterm elections were. After talking with hundreds of people that thought they knew everything about Midterm Elections, I found that there was more to this often overlooked voting opportunity than meets the eye. First of all, those that vote midterm had more power than they ever realized. Voters who vote, and perhaps even those who don't are responsible for keeping so many incumbents in office for too long. Midterm elections minimally keep the same two-thirds of Congress in office. Midterms are like an "off season" for voting, so polls have very low turnouts because people are not aware of the importance of these elections. The key point to understand is that Midterm Elections are a crucial step in changing one-third of Congress every even-numbered year! Besides replacing the 33 Senators whose seats expire they could replace *all* 435 Representatives of the House. This fact may be obvious to some, but it is of vital importance to let all voters know this bit of information.

If we share with others the importance and power that midterm elections have over our lives, we have a much better chance of making this change happen in the next twenty years. The word, "midterm" literally means the halfway point of a President's term. During this time, we could potentially elect 33 or 34 new Senators. Imagine how the legislature would change as a result. For example, in the 2018 midterm elections, 33 "new" Class I Senators can potentially be elected, effectively changing the course of Congress and legislation. Then in 2020, it's likely a president will have a second term and 33 "new" Class II Senators. Between 2016 and 2020, we can replace all 100 Senators and House Representatives.

Such a paramount change would give a President that was elected for a second term a new House and a new Senate. It would provide us with an entirely new Congress that could start reviewing, removing, and rescinding the unneeded legislation. What's interesting is that in 2022, if we are unhappy with the changes that we have made, we get a second chance to use the mighty midterm elections to replace the 34 Class III Senators that we replaced in 2016 or the ones that we missed in 2016.

Now can you see why midterm elections were actually set up? Midterm elections are as important to the people as the presidential election is to the party. The more power the party can build up the longer their incumbents can stay in office. Approximately 40% of eligible voters come out to vote during midterm elections, as compared to 60% during presidential elections.[27]

## Showing Compassion

*Instead of working against each other and judging others about their incomplete knowledge of the constitution, we must work together by sharing and teaching the power of working for a common goal. Voters who choose to represent their opinions via violent protests are placing themselves on the wrong side of the law, which denies them the right to gather peacefully in the future.*

*Showing a little compassion for each person's point of view will ensure that we all continue to have the freedom to voice our opinion. Our country was built on the foundation of free speech. Instead of anger aimed at the opposing party or anyone with a different viewpoint, let's put our energy into using the prescription to healing Congress that was outlined in the Constitution. Spread the word, and vote out any politician who has been in office six years or longer.*

## Stubbornness

The party system represents itself visually and vividly in iconic reds and blues, with elephants and donkeys everywhere. Not ironically, elephants and donkeys are two animals that are notoriously difficult to move due to their stubborn nature. When taking our history into consideration, it seems quite appropriate that these two animals have been chosen as the icons to represent our two immovable giants - the Republican and Democratic parties. The reality is that they don't represent the people's government any more than do long-term politicians. Stubborn and immovable are two adjectives that are interchangeable between both a determined conservative or liberal voter.

We are reminded once again how our selected officials have lost track of the fundamentals our government was built on. Due to the decision making of America's Congress, we have uncontrolled borders, loss of wages, fewer benefits and jobs altogether, disproportionately higher cost of living expenses, loss of freedom, human rights including privacy and the millions of people dealing with hunger in the United States every year.

## This Is A Silent Plea To All Voters For Not Having Career Politicians

Every two years when it comes time to vote, the two major parties appear to have unwavering confidence with their incumbents. And we wonder why more people don't vote. Why should anyone vote if the party has already done it for them? The game is simple: the more seats any given party has in the House or Senate, the more control they have over the Legislative Branch as a whole.

They can then choose an incumbent president to implement their pre-formulated agendas. What's worse is that we pay them generously to behave this way, supplementing their lavish lifestyle with bonus benefits and a few million dollars each for their "operation" budget. When they misbehave, instead of voting these crooks out of office, we refrain from voting entirely (just as good as re-electing them back into office) and wave our hand at the problem thinking that the solution is not within reach.

There is something fundamentally wrong with this type of thinking. Our inflexibility to change and blindness to reason is leading us further down the rabbit hole to an uncertain future. We can't accomplish anything unless we attempt to work together. We must focus our attention on taking back our power and right as a people to truly elect our lawmakers and representatives. If an incumbent cannot get re-elected, special interest groups or PAC's can't buy their vote. Getting PAC money out of government will go a long way in returning America to her true purpose: being a land of freedom and opportunity.

# Chapter Ten

## Term Limits Are Up To The Voters & Not Congress

Have you ever said to yourself, "Shouldn't we have term limits?" or, "Why don't we have better choices of candidates?" Perhaps you've said, "I thought once elected they were going to make government smaller, have fewer wars, lower our taxes, have a better health-care system, have a better education system, and less corruption in government"?

All of these phenomena would necessitate an "Act of Congress." Neither party that has had the majority seats or control of Congress has accomplished these tasks, nor is it in their best interest to do so. Their small talk is cheap rhetoric -- or should we say easy – because when Congress speaks, it's in trillions of "borrowed" dollars. I hate to say it, but the larger your budget, the more important you seem. We know there is a better way - and our term limits don't need today's Congress to refine or amend them. Voters just need to vote.

Ben Franklin had a novel way of making decisions. He used to draw a line in the center of a sheet of paper, making two columns. On one side he wrote "yes" and the other "no." He would then ask himself several questions with a list of yes and no answers. The list with the most check marks would indicate how he should make a decision – either leaning towards "yes," or towards " no."

Most of us would have marked more "yes" for term limits, better candidates, smaller government, less war, lower taxes, better healthcare, better education, and less corruption. So if our current Congress hasn't made any of these happen, shouldn't it be clear to vote them out? The answer is "yes" as it's common sense and it's based on reason.

Taxes continue to increase monthly. An example anyone can relate

73

to is the taxes and fees line on your phone bill – the same line you will find on your Internet, cable TV, medical, and electrical bill. Government adds taxes to all of the above, plus the cost to record and store, all phone calls, all sent and received emails, all websites viewed or referenced and everything we put on Facebook, Twitter, LinkedIn or the Cloud.

These could be called vampire taxes, as they are being sucked out of you by a third party and paid to the government. Most of your tax money is funding the very agencies that oversee the companies that are benefiting from these taxes. What does this mean? Here's an example; you pay a certain amount of taxes on your phone bill. The telecom company pays this money to the Federal Communications Commission (FCC), a regulatory body that is supposed to keep telecommunications companies in check. Broadband providers can also track, collect, and share information about your physical location, your financial problems, and chronic medical conditions in real time. The FCC has submitted a proposal to protect the sharing of this personal data as recently as March of 2016. The verdict is yet unknown. [28] Other companies that generate almost all of their revenue from getting the inside scoop into your personal life have absolutely no monitoring or regulation in the United States at this time. Such companies include giants like Google, Yahoo, and Facebook.

Both, common sense and reasoning are not taught in any regular schools, colleges or universities. I have used it throughout this book with the hope that some **Sense** sinks in and you have found the **Reason** to use it. If Congress had common sense they would know America's huge debt doesn't make sense without a plan to pay it back, wouldn't they?'

The concept is identical to the process of requesting a personal or business loan. The bank will want to see your assets as collateral to leverage the risk of your loan, but most importantly they will ask for a contingency plan for paying back the funds.

They will want answers to simple questions, like whether you have a steady job, and whether your income is sufficient to repay the loan according to specific terms and requirements. Should you default on your loan, you must give up something of equal value – like your home. Similarly, when our country requires a loan, reason dictates that we must be able to show our ability to repay that money. If Congress insists that the repayment terms are being drafted but refuse to disclose the terms, we are forced to conclude that something is being covered up. Long-term congressmen and women have been operating this way for as long as most of us can remember, and they teach this irresponsible behavior to new members. That's **Reason** enough to change officials, as that l ne of thinking doesn't make any **Sense.**

Counter to popular belief, a tax increase is not the only method to manage our budget. A reduction in the cost of running government will have an agreeable impact with long-term healing benefits. In other words, spend less money and the money you do spend, spend it carefully; use forethought and common sense to reduce expenses. **Note to politicians**: read and understand the bill before you pass it!

# Chapter Eleven

## The People's Term Limits

*"We cannot solve our problems with the same thinking we used when we created them."*

*-Albert Einstein*

The finality of term limits and what that concept truly means for our government and country is like a law that was never written. It is vital that we share this concept with as many people as possible in order *to promote voting for* non-incumbents in *both midterm and presidential elections. So who should* we *vote for? It's not about telling* people what party or candidate *to vote for; it's about the method of implementing term-limits* for *Congress.*

*It's important to understand that if we don't start to implement* these concepts, we are setting our government up for failure.

Let's break down the numbers concretely to make the decision as easy as possible. In November of each even-numbered year, we can vote to replace part of Congress. The first opportunity to do so is coming up this November 2016, when 34 states will have an opportunity to vote out 34 Class III Senators. Sixteen states will have to wait for the next opportunity in two or four years, depending on their cycle. In 2016, all fifty states will have a chance to use their term-limiting power on all four hundred and thirty-five (435) members of the House of Representatives. Check the index at the end of this book to see whom not to vote for in your district this year.

In November 2018, 33 states get their opportunity to vote out 33 Class I Senators while 17 states take a back seat. Again all fifty states have a second chance to use their term-limiting power on the House Representatives.

In November 2020, the third portion (33 in total, just as before) of Senators known as Class II can be voted out of Congress. The complete list of all three classes of senators by state and their respective year of class expiry is available at the end of the book. The compiled catalog for 2016 is included for your convenience as well. Should we follow this simple formula, we will achieve the true meaning of the people's term-limits.

At least every four years a U.S. Senator from our state reaches the expiration date of their class. Every two years all House Representatives could also be replaced. It follows that at least one vote every two years for a senator and two votes every two years for a House Rep combine to create the perfect algorithm for new talent in Congress.

On the senate.gov website, the words "class" and "term" are clearly explained:

"Article I, section 3 of the Constitution requires the Senate to be divided into three classes for purposes of elections. Senators are elected to six-year terms, and every two years the members of one class— approximately one-third of the senators—face election or reelection.  Terms for senators in Class I expire in 2019, Class II in 2021, and Class III in 2017."[29]

This straightforward passage may come as a surprise to someone who has never heard the mention of classes and term limits during election years. Furthermore, this government website also gives the background and history to how senatorial classes were first chosen, and why;

"On the morning of May 15, 1789, Tristram Dalton climbed the steep stairs to the Senate chamber in New York City's Federal Hall. At a few minutes after 11 a.m., the recently elected Massachusetts senator placed his hand into a small wooden box. With Vice President John Adams presiding and 12 of the Senate's 20 members looking on, Dalton grasped a small slip of paper and lifted it for all to see. He then read its brief notation: "Number One." With that ritual act, seven senators became members of "Class One" and learned that their terms of office would expire within two years."[30]

## How Illegal Immigrants Help Legislators Stay in Office

There are a number of reasons why people want to immigrate to the United States. Whether someone immigrates to the US legally or illegally, they come here for the one thing that we've taken for granted – *freedom*. Yes, they also take advantage of the American system, using social programs for their benefit. These programs have cost trillions of dollars, and yet Congress does not seem to have good solutions to remedy such massive cost. In turn, the legislative body creates more laws, more agencies, and ever more powerful policing actions that impact existing citizens. Meanwhile, the legal citizens of America are just thrown into the mix of "all people," thereby losing more of our citizenship rights in the process.

Illegal immigrants are counted in our census but don't have the rights to vote. Legislators take advantage of the immigrant count – legal or not – because the size of their constituency directly impacts the number of representatives assigned to each district.[31] Most countries enforce a passport or occupancy law. If you don't have a passport and the right visa don't enter because if caught, you will be fined, forced to leave, and probably not allowed to return for some time.[33]

# Cost Per Illegal In The United States

The United States funnels trillions of borrowed dollars to feeding, housing, educating, providing medical services to, and employing illegal immigrants. Plus we pay interest on that money.

The cost per illegal immigrant is rising in the United States. The government (and therefore taxpayer) pay for education (number of teachers, salaries, pensions, & classrooms), insurance [non-insured motorist cost], use of resources (jobs, healthcare, roads, housing, energy, police, used vehicles that citizens need, signage, instructions, prisons), to name a few.

The Federation for American Immigration Reform published a report in 2013 titled, *The Fiscal Burden of Illegal Immigrants in the United States.* The report estimates that there around 13 million undocumented immigrants in the United States, costing taxpayers around $113 billion a year. Education is the largest expense. It costs America $52 billion a year to send illegal immigrant children to school.[33]

The overwhelming daily cost surpasses $309,589,000. For every six years in office, we spend $678 billion dollars so that illegal immigrants can continue to live here and take advantage of our freedom. The numbers are staggering, but what can be done? Congress has spent more time in the last 50 years creating ways to have more control over its own citizens than it has creating solutions to deal with the illegal immigration problem. The idea of building a wall around the United States is incomprehensible. Nonetheless, the cost to build one could be easily reimbursed by the money that we don't spend on illegal immigrants – should we finally choose to bar them from living in this country on our dime.

# With Larger Populations...

The number of rules, restrictions, and laws required to maintain a safe environment in our society is derived as a direct correlation to the number of people in a given area. Reason would dictate that with a larger population (comprised of legal or illegal residents), it becomes more expensive for the government to manage infrastructure and enforce law and order. Law and order are harder to implement when the population does not understand English, does not know or understand the local and federal laws, and does not understand or respect American culture. The outcome affects you and your family directly.

The money that must be diverted to address and care for illegal immigrants results in higher cost for our health care and education systems as we pick up illegals. Costs rise when illegals use our natural resources, transportation system, law enforcement, and legal system. These all come at a tremendous expense and either take away from or inconveniences our freedom. Instead of addressing the problem head on, Congress uses the hot-button issue as a tool to their benefit - justifying the creation of a variety of agencies that in turn come with a slew of self-inflicted regulations. Other countries have come up with solutions such as better border protection and deportation of illegal immigrants. The United States, on the other hand, uses the trickle down affect where Federal Government mandates new regulations that impact every citizen in every state. The state applies it to each county, the county reflects on each township, and your township brings it to your neighborhood; then your neighborhood committee tells *you* they are going to raise property taxes.

How often do you hear someone asking the question, "Why do we have so many laws?" The more people physically reside in our country, the more laws we will have as there is less to share and a smaller space to do it within. Again, this is **common sense**.

80

From this, we derive the following four lessons/**reasons**: 1) Vote out those that write more restrictions and unjust law; 2) Do it sooner than later; 3) Send illegal immigrants home; and 4) Add a simple addendum that your parents need to be U.S. citizens before you are a natural born citizen of the United States. This amendment is so simple, yet impactful. We would need the minimum vote of 38 states to make the necessary change to the 14th Amendment, and I believe that it is possible.

In the true words of one of our vice presidents, in his August 1996 speech at the Democratic National Convention,

*"We Americans write our own history. And the chapters of which we're proudest are the ones where we had the courage to change. Time and again, Americans have seen the need for change, and have taken the initiative to bring that change to life."* Al Gore

It's important to think of the impact that term limits would have from a worldwide perspective. If leaders of all countries had a maximum of six years in office, could there be as many wars? If we truly implemented the laws that have been outlined in our Constitution, it would be nearly impossible for the United States to start another conflict.

By replacing them with new public servants every two years, the legislative body would not have the ability or enough power to go to war. Being attacked or defending our country's borders is different than being the aggressor. Implementing a significant military action like declaring war in Iraq is completely unacceptable. FYI, how many times have we been told by our existing government that we would be withdrawing 100% of our troops from Iraq, Afghanistan, Iran, Syria, Turkey, Pakistan, etc. without ever fulfilling that promise, A Google search will reveal that the last time we did what we said was under President Thomas Jefferson. He learned quickly that these were wars that we were meddling in were based on passions and anger over religion and could never truly be won.

# Chapter Twelve

## "Six Years & Out" - Our New Mantra

"Six Years & Out" is a simple rule of thumb that's easy to remember and easy to say.  Try saying it out loud; sounds pretty good doesn't it?  Keep in mind that Senators and Representatives don't have a boss, a manager or any supervision. They even have immunity to several laws that they have personally written. This may keep them in their unrealistic bubble once they are voted into office but how does it make the volunteers feel that helped them get re-elected? It seems that we are not genuinely looking for a strong leader, but a way to support a party agenda. If the opposing candidate pertained to your party would you have had the same thoughts? There is only one answer! The answer is that the person who can do a better job is the one we should ever consider voting for.

## Putting Your Loyalty in the Right Place

Completing a six-year duration should be a fulfilling and a definitive measurement of success for every public official (unless a different term limit applies to their specific office). Once they are elected, it should be an exhausting job for them to work together in achieving the wants and desires of their constituents and continuously striving to do that which is best for America. Anyone that has ever sat on a Board of Directors understands it is a thankless job and can't wait to complete his or her term and take the first exit out. Contrary to this logic, politicians want to stay in office. The idea is a quagmire.

If only the above were true. Instead, the two parties always fight each other and spend a lot of time strategizing how to stay in office.  How have the volunteers been able to keep that in perspective knowing incumbent Senators or Representatives are making $174,000 a year to campaign?

Are we that devoted to aligning ourselves with a specific party and willing to allow this to occur for the duration of our lifetime of voting?

Party blindness is in direct conflict with the goal of replacing incumbents with new people. Supporting incumbents is involuntarily supporting the faults that any Congress may have. What they also have in common is their joint support of a broken portion of government – that is Congress as a whole. Their loyalty is to the party, and we are looking for patriots that are loyal to America and the people.

If a volunteer has apprehensions about this concept, it's because they cannot let go of the well-engrained old voting system and propaganda that has been drilled into the voters' minds and hearts. We have followed this erroneous system like Sheeple, (Sheeple *are people who tend to follow the majority in matters of opinion and are easily persuaded).* It is time to use our sense and reason and follow the Constitutional approach to voting.

Congress has failed to uphold the oath of the Constitution and be united in working together towards a common goal. Instead, both parties work for the good of the party and the good of super PAC contributors and have lured volunteers or Sheeple to do the same. In fact, isn't it dishonest that they have all made wages of over one million forty-four thousand dollars each six years of being office while continuing to campaign throughout their term? They've had fun at our cost; now it's time for the "good 'ole boys club" to go.

If we don't change whom we elect into office, how will the culture of our representation ever change? Our legislators have zero accountability for productivity measures such as positive performance, the growth of our economy, social stability, and the creation of real jobs. Despite the lack of performance metrics; these same legislators get pay increases after elections. Do you remember voting on their pay or benefits?

Reminiscent of our broken banking system, our congressmen have actually created the 28th Constitutional Amendment that mandates their raise! You might ask, "How is this possible?" The dilemma is that Constitutional Amendments are not brought to the people for review, although they conclusively public information!

Sometime in the future when we have a new Congress that is elected by the people, we will be able to see public bills before they become Federal Law. It's quite clear that Congress, as it exists now, should not be passing any new amendments to the Constitution. It is within our rights to demand that all amendments should come back to the people to either pass or turn down.

A friend of mine said it well; Congress has literally lost the art and desire for a "will to do good" and with that, a will to do it with a conscious effort. They have honed the skill of not taking responsibility and blaming someone else for the problems that are created as a direct result of the bad legislature. They don't seem to understand that when they make unjust laws, they are not laws at all. To continue to make thousands of laws without removing those that are outdated or violate our Rights is Constitutionally illegal.

# Chapter Thirteen

## The Ten-Year Rule

Once we have career politicians out of office, we should think about having an unwritten requirement of staying out of politics for at least ten years. The term, "out of politics" should mean that the individual abstains from all variations of consecutive rounds of public office. Keeping them out of office for ten years would allow our country to move forward and strengthen our system of democracy. Keeping this rhythm will also prevent politicians from being continuously supported by PACs. Implementing the Mantra of "Six Years & Out" along with a "Ten Years Out" Rule may be just the combination that keeps career politicians from disrupting newly elected officials.

It would be interesting to see how or if PAC money would exist. If PACs continue to endure, how they would spend their money knowing that incumbents won't be re-elected? Can you imagine a super PAC spending millions of dollars on advertising just in the hope that someone gets re-elected? We know this is happening now as incumbents are constantly looking for campaign money. We suffer the pain from the inadequacy of both Houses of Congress with much of the blame caused by their campaigning.

Nonetheless, PAC campaign money along with party-line voting has been effective in convincing American Sheeple for the last two hundred years to vote along the party line.

If politicians were kept out of office for ten years, they could potentially improve their eligibility to be reelected by actively partaking in the real world. They would see how their legislature and or lack of service have impacted the United States and the world. To create the possibility of an improved political infrastructure would ironically take an act of our current Congress, aka the "lawmakers," to write an Amendment.

Then they would have to pass it and have it approved by 38 states to make it a Constitutional law.

We don't want that kind of law, written by any Congress for at least the next eight years. It would take away another freedom from the Republic to run this country. The dangers of today's Congress to have the ability to change any part of the Constitution should be worrisome to all Americans.

In doing this research, I have read a few Constitutions from other countries. Some were quite disheartening and a word of caution to America, other countries may have used the United States Constitution as a guide, but their leaders have slanted it to their legislative advantage. Their legislation has the power and ability to denounce the peoples' interest with words like "unless or according to the statute..." which limits, restricts or abolishes those rights.

The wording that includes such limitations should signal a red flag for the people who have sworn to uphold the Constitution. The fact is that we have federal laws that limit and even abolish our rights as United States citizens. These laws, along with 13,000 executive orders from our past and current presidents, are all designed to control the governed. It is, therefore, integral that if any amendments are to be written or changed, we need to make sure they come back to the people to vote on and not legislation.

Reading other countries' Constitutions opened my eyes to just how powerful this document is and how our Constitution is one of the greatest ever written. The US Constitution was written to declare that a government should be for the people and by the people. We need to be doing the choosing of whom we are entrusting that power to, and currently, we're not selecting our true representatives. If an incumbent is attempting to get re-elected, a yellow flag needs to go up until the party provides us with more than one candidate for the same position.

## People Can Pass Amendments Into Law

The power of the people to amend the Constitution is written in Article V of the United States Constitution. Nonetheless, it has only happened once in 225 years – that was in 1933 when the Twenty-First Amendment was approved. The Twenty-First Amendment rescinded the Eighteenth Amendment that prohibited manufacturing, selling, or transportaticn of alcohol in the US. The Eighteenth Amendment is the only Constitutional amendment that has ever been repealed. It was brought to the people for approval and replaced by the Twenty-First Amendment. Now, you have the freedom to have a drink - either before, after, or while you are reading this incredibly interesting book.............................

# Chapter Fourteen

## American Royalty

Over the last 250 years, we find that legislation has taken great strides in putting restraints on how and whom we vote for. In some bizarre sort of way, we have our own form of royalty that was created and nurtured by our government. We seem to allow family member after family member to grow up to become our leaders. Either the families' party or their aligned super PACs have succeeded in aiding some families destined to perennial dependence on public support. A Yale study shows that *"Political dynasties, exemplify a particular form of elite persistence in which a single or few family groups monopolize political power. Political dynasties are common in many contemporary democracies such as Argentina, India, Japan, Mexico, the Philippines and to some extent in the United States."*

The study also suggests that "incumbency advantage may spill over to their family members, or they may even carry it with them to races for other offices."[34]

## Who Are They?

Political dynasties are by no means an occurrence that escapes the United States, with ubiquitous names like Roosevelt, Kennedy, Clinton, Gore, Rockefeller, Daley, Bush, Kerry, Cheney and possibly Obama again in 2024. These names are recognized as readily in the household as in the political sphere. In 2016, we had both the Clinton and the Bush family trying once again to get control of the presidency. Bush dropped out in 2016, but the name is still there for future reference. For better or worse, we seem to allow family member after family member to grow up to become a politician.

In some cases, the husband or wife of a past leader may be elected to a legislative office down the line.

Remember, it's all about political power, special privileges, and control that drives the desire for office for each member of these famous families. It is frowned upon when a medical doctor wants to treat his or her family member for illness. There is no law against voting family members into political office; it's not immoral but is questionable whether it looks more like a monarchy form of government. Our natural instinct should tell us that this does not serve the best interest of America.

If we were given the freedom to choose non-incumbents for office, would family members even make it to the list of top-ten candidates? We will never know unless we change the way we think about voting. Why are we allowing family members to embody the single "best" option for the candidates for any official post?

Article One of the Constitution clearly set guidelines so that we would replace one-third of Senators, one class at a time. We must take those guidelines to heart and discontinue voting for incumbents or a political family that were in office for six years or longer.

If we follow the Constitution as we are meant to, new names will surface as candidates for Senatorial seats every two years. Think of the Constitution as an experimental guide that has left it up to us to refine how the government would be run. Upon reviewing the results of this experiment, we will discover an inescapable truth; the analysis clearly proves that leaving people in office longer than six years doesn't work. We need to overcome thoughts such as, "But, [insert your favorite incumbent or bureaucrats name] has been doing a good job", or, "[insert incumbent name] has been better than most, so they can stay in office". If we all think this way, all the warnings in the world regarding name recognition [American Royalty] will never make a difference.

We have to look at the greater problem and need at hand, and follow a basic rule to keep our political system functioning smoothly.

Bureaucrats are all supposed to be public servants. One can easily imagine how a long-running politician might gain too much insider information, power, and sway over other members of Congress. Imagine how that political weight can be augmented when it is passed on to their family members. A look into George H.W. Bush's political career reveals how intimately involved he was in many major political decisions on Capitol Hill, even before ever gaining the presidential seat. Bush had the unique advantage of serving as the Director of Central Intelligence and being on the receiving end of that intelligence as President. What strikes me as a particularly good example of insider politics is the personalized attention and help that G.H.W. afforded to Carter before the incumbent was even named as a candidate for presidency. Bush briefed Carter on many sensitive and highly classified topics to give him the advantage of a level playing field when debating with President Ford during elections.[54] Inside information is just that, information that no one else has. The CIA can find out whatever they want about anyone without question. Federal agencies run the government not the other way around.

Take a moment and reflect on any agencies you can think of. Do you think our legislation has any control or power over them? If so, this would be in the news every day. We don't want career politicians, career bureaucrats and certainly not families staying in politics and retaining all the control over all events in our country. Unlike a family business, an oligarchy is a dangerous game for a democratic country.

# Chapter Fifteen

## There is No Hidden Agenda in *How To Replace Congress*

The agenda is to teach as many people as possible the concept that one-third of Congress can be replaced every two years. This thought movement is for anyone that believes in the virtues of our country and wants the United States to remain the greatest country in the world. It has to start with a change in how we think and talk about politics. We have to be able to share this information in as many ways and to as many different people and lifestyles as possible. The result is that we are making an effort towards regaining our rights - starting with our right to vote.

We need a voting system that is beyond the parties', legislators' or any single state's control. It needs to be a voting system that is set up Constitutionally for having the freedom of whom we vote for. The ballot should not limit the voter to a party or a side, but rather show all the candidates that are running for office. We deserve a voting system that truly shows us that the United States is a republic, where the people choose legislators of the governed. We must return to our roots, and nourish a republic where leaders have a maximum term of six years in public office. While in office, these leaders must serve the greater good of the country, not their biggest investor or personal interests. They remove laws that negatively impact our Rights. We need new ideas and to share them in how we can improve America. This voting system needs to be controlled for the people by the legislation we are entrusting those powers to. This Congress and these parties have failed America by keeping incumbents in office.

# A Spending Society Supports A Thriving And Growing Economy

Jobs are created when people have more money to spend. The more money that is spent, the more jobs are created. For the last 20 years, our jobs and our money have been moving out of America. In 2008, the number of jobs in America plummeted, leaving our workforce with a loss of 40% of their net worth. Repair is needed and is not going to happen with the same Congress that allowed our jobs and our factories to move out of America. To put this in perspective, do you wait for 34 failing bridges to collapse before continuing to drive over water? Or do you put together a plan and replace all 34 of them before anyone can come to harm?

**A Few Ideas For Putting America Back To Work [No Specific Order]**

1) Broadband America [see the Broadband America Act of 2009]

2) Change from centralized generation to local distributed generation

3) Implement a Demand Side Management Energy Mandate

4) Waste water run-off and water treatment program for America

5) Rebuild our broken Highway & Bridge infrastructure

6) A Presidential Call for a cure for cancer in five years

7) Restructure, Rescind, Reinforce immigration laws in "America"

8) Reform – Insurance companies, Oil companies, Tel-cons, Pharmaceuticals, Medical in general, Financial industry & more

9) Remove restrictions & encumbrances for corporations to grow

10) Bring back or tax the outsourcing of customer service jobs that are given away by U.S. owned corporations

11) Encourage to buy American and fix our broken trade agreements

## The Truth Will Set You Free

Political propaganda has us believing many things. One of the most common lies that we are told about voting is that voting for any candidate other than a Republican or a Democrat is a waste of a vote. Could this be a convenient invention that was designed to make us feel as though our vote cannot make a difference? Remember we talked about the importance of knowing what not to do earlier? Instead of voting in the same incumbents we should vote for new, fresh leadership. Everything you've learned in this book has hopefully given you a better understanding and a deeper respect for our Constitution.

These are our original Rights in The Declaration of Independence that we fought for in order to allow America to become a country. Our forefathers had the wisdom of putting them in writing. We need to not only re-learn these Rights we need to use those Rights for the good of all. The Constitution is what gives all of us individual rights, liberty, and the theory of limited government.

It also gives us our natural rights and a government with sovereignty [consent by the people and where the people have supreme power through democracy and ability to replace its government constitutionally [a government that protects the human rights of all citizens].

If you vote, please take a step back and see how our voting system has been structured to benefit each party, keep legislators in office, restrict associations and unions from talking about incumbents 60 days before elections, and ultimately stop any religious group from talking or writing how they are politically being governed. All of these restrictions become harder to withstand as additional laws are written and passed that take away our rights and freedoms. Our borders have been left open to allow other countries' immigrants to come to the US for a chance at a better life. When our kindness is taken for granted, and our laws are broken and abused, we cannot allow people to enter our land until they comply with our societal standards and rules.

# Chapter Sixteen

## When America Was Great

**Special Note:** Individuals under the age of 45 may never experience the true freedom and security that are within our rights as citizens of America because these rights have been hidden or stolen from the people over a matter of decades. Are they lost to us forever?

1). **America was;** a place where - Airline tickets were like cash. You could use your ticket the day you were scheduled to fly; use it on that airline or another carrier; use it in six months, or even fly somewhere else; you could even give it to a friend even though your name was on it. It was better than cash. You could park outside the airport and bring your luggage inside. You could bring as much luggage as you wanted without all the extra fees. You got served a great breakfast, lunch or dinner on your flight at no charge. You could bring a friend or family member to the gate, or they could wait at the gate while your plane was landing. You could even buy a ticket the day you were flying and sometimes even at the gate before the plane was going to leave. **Is this what you would like or stick with the TSA's new restrictions on the way we fly?**

2). **America was;** a place where **almost everything was made in America**, and it was good. All your clothes, shoes, cars, TVs, electronics, steel, copper, even sheet rock. Corporate raiders gave those jobs away and blamed much of it on the Unions! There was a time when if you wanted to change jobs, you could, as there were plenty of better-paying jobs that had a choice of benefits. **Corporate greed expressed via our legislators in Congress allowed for limitations on movement and job creation.**

3).     **America was;** where you could call any company and expect **a person to answer the phone** "every time," **speak clear English,** and be on site in the United States. You didn't have to listen to a foreign language, a robotic voice, or "press 1 for English". **These customer service jobs should be brought back to America, and only Congress can make that happen.**

4).     **America was a safe place to mail a letter** or to go to the library and read a book in privacy. The library was a safe place for your children to go. The post office never opened your mail, and never copied it under the strict orders of the government. Federal agencies did not invade the privacy of your home every single day, listening to your private phone calls and conversations, reading your emails, and monitoring your every move. **Do we feel safer and more secure with DHS & other federal laws that we're unaware of?** The answer is NO!

5).     **America was** a safe place to live. Our military didn't "mysteriously" lose 1200 surface to air missiles and then "coincidentally" open borders from Mexico to the United States that very same month. All the TSA airport security in the world can't make flying safely with even one of those missiles in somebody's hands! **Maybe they should have a traffic camera on their weapons storage and transfer. Jeez!** How many jets have already been shot down?

6).     **America's Government;** didn't force companies to give up secure information on their customers (Apple is one example). **The Patriotic Act, along with DHS created a great loss of freedom and the degradation of America's true identity.**

7).     **America's Government;** was not a government that declared WAR on other Countries, unless they declared war on us first. The American war in Iraq is one example of using our tax dollars to wage war without an explanation. **There are numerous non-violent solutions to** many of our country's problems. We could avoid conflict and the death of our brave young soldiers if we just use sense and reason.

8).     **Freedom was; having a lower cost choice for a vehicle;** Technology has created many conveniences and woes in the last fifty years. Cars controlled by computers - from headlights to dashboard TVs, and backup cameras, to remote controlled parking – have increased the base cost of a standard car by four times of what it was before. For the younger generation, this is a major issue. **PAC money and an unchanging Congress is the problem.** We should have the ability to shut them off.

9).     **Freedom was; having safe water and food** that was not genetically altered. The town of Flint, Michigan is an early indicator of this major problem with fresh water. Thanks to mercury and acid rain caused by coal-fired power plants, as well as out-of-control pollution from our vehicles and agriculture, we no longer have clean air to breathe. True, we have put controls on pollution from coal-fired power plants in the U.S., but the biggest offenders continue to evade regulation due to conflict of interest from PACs.

10).     **Freedom was; going to a doctor and getting treatment and results without having to check with your insurance company, and go to countless other doctors to collect referrals to satisfy your insurance carrier.** Emergency medical treatments are through the roof, and staying one night at the hospital will cost you more money than the most luxurious all-inclusive hotel in the world. The broken insurance system has pushed patients and doctors to previously unthinkable limits. **In some states, (i.e. Florida) medical doctors are not required to carry malpractice insurance; they have you sign a document that waives your rights to sue them for malpractice.** FYI, don't get a bladder infection on the weekend. It has to be Monday-Friday 7 am- 5 pm.

11).    **Freedom was; feeling safe in your home;** if you had a dog in your house and the dog met you at the door, your home was safe. **Today government is in you home, recording your phone calls, recording whatever your reading on the Internet, allow for back doors to be on your computers so they can be hacked.**

12).    **Freedom was; when TV was free,** when you could have multiple phones on the same line when Internet was going to be Wi-Fi throughout America. **Telecoms have been deregulated and have most people believing that we still need them. We don't.**

13).    **Freedom was; being safe walking down the sidewalk;** without a hoodie, because you didn't want the world following you around with street and traffic cameras. **The Department of Homeland Security and others have infinite storage of your actions and whereabouts.**

14).    **Freedom would be; knowing that taking synthetically made medications is unhealthy** for the human body; that being exposed to radiation creates a higher risk of developing cancer; that the AMA and FDA and medical insurance need massive reforming. **If PACs are keeping legislators in office for over six years, this will never be done.**

15)    **Not being stalked by companies because your phone has a GPS in it.** You parked in a banks lot for a few minutes now it shows up on your computer or phone to open an account with that bank!

16).    **Americans think we should let someone else's kids fix our problems. This is the predicted party-line voter's response to the suggestion that we must begin to make the needed changes today.**

> All Sixteen of these freedoms we no longer have and never been should have been taken away from us. It is time to shake up the trend of fear-based control from Congress terrorist groups and now businesses, all trying to control our lives.

# Chapter Seventeen

## Learning a Lifelong Skill

*"People who work together will win, whether it be against complex football defenses or the problems of modern society."*

*- Vince Lombardi*

Utilizing the power of consensus is a learned behavior and an effective method of problem solving while using common sense. Learning this important skill can help us in all aspects of decision-making in our lives. Consensus gives way to majority rule, but also allows each person to present his or her point of view or solution for consideration.

Resolution through consensus is about allowing new ideas to come forward and building on those ideas to create positive change for yourself, your family, your town, and even your country. When we take ourselves out of the voting process, we allow others to control our lives and our freedoms. We become resigned to the idea that there is nothing we can do to change the way things are. In fact, this could not be farther from the truth. Most communities find solutions to their problems and needs by voting to determine consensus.

Voting or not voting, as we mentioned earlier, is a personal choice. Individual common sense should have us all voting. If not, you're letting your neighbor's votes run your life. Voting is seen as a challenge because deciding whom to vote for often seems impossible. To make it easy, just vote for anyone who is not already an incumbent. This is the first step toward limiting the potential for someone else to run your life. Many people align themselves with one party or another, and those parties have been running our lives.

99

Our forefathers used the consensus vote in order to find common ground among dozens of ideas and decisions that went into the creation of our Declaration of Independence and Constitution. The same method was used to create the Bill of Rights. Our rights have since been infringed upon in countless ways, such as the gag order issued by Lyndon Johnson that we discussed in Chapter Four, and the McCain-Feingold act that we reviewed in Chapter Five. The McCain-Feingold Act is promoted as a non-partisan bill, but it should be called the "Pro-Incumbent" Bill as it has nothing to do with being nonpartisan and everything to do with helping politicians stay in office. Again, voting by consensus would enable all unions, corporations, and churches to get part of their First Amendment back.

The moment that a politician is elected to office, they inevitably stop thinking for themselves because they are forced to follow their party's agenda. That is pretty much the way it works; if the newbie doesn't follow the party (for or against their better judgment), they will never get the opportunity to introduce any of their ideas or new bills into Congress. The party leaders do the thinking and talking for them.

When the newbies do think for themselves, they think about what they have to do to stay in office. The candidate or incumbent that you voted for has to spend most of his or her political career pandering to the party leaders who have been in office for over six years. Due to this myopic way of limiting the incumbents' thoughts and actions, it's up to voters to keep fresh minds in Congress. If this voting method had been used every two years since the inception of the Constitution, we would have steadily improved government and its efficiency. Instead, we have had the exact opposite. So through a consensus voting system, we can start replacing one-third of Congress every two years, which will be a start for the needed changes that only a new Congress can give us.

It may shock you to hear that not a single United States President has been elected by the people in over 228 years. In the last two decades, George W. Bush was *selected* twice, even though he lost the popular vote. We continue to use an Electoral College system or each state's legislators to choose who is going to be the next president of the United States. This election year of 2016 is another example of how legislation is tremendously impacting the presidential candidates. Only time will tell how these candidates will choose to run for or from their party. Once the dust has settled, we will have to wait to see who the Electoral College will choose to be president in 2016.

There were four influences that worked in the best interest for George W. Bush in becoming president. Remember, he was not elected but "selected" twice. Bush had the following four strengths: 1) He is American Royalty [Bush Family]; 2) The outdated Electoral College worked in his favor; 3) The questionable Super PACs and special interest money supported his platform, and; 4) Party-line voting swayed the odds in his favor because no other Republican came out on top.

Debt and war have been two sons of George W.'s legacy as president. During his time in office, Congress approved trillions of dollars in American debt; our country entered into several ongoing military conflicts via Executive Order, America's infrastructure was left to fall apart, and the price of oil skyrocketed [no surprise with a Bush being in office]. Nevertheless, most of our existing Congress didn't challenge another president gone wild.

# Chapter Eighteen

## An Honest Politician May Not Stay Honest Very Long

Once elected into office, a politician often finds it difficult to stay faithful to the promises they made and agenda they laid out during the election. The reason is not due to their innately corrupt character or scheming nature (although undoubtedly some politicians do fall into this category). Indeed, the very system of government that has been established on Capitol Hill conspires in every way to limit the individual representative's freedom of speech and vote and manipulates him or her quite deliberately to follow the party's general prerogative. Why'd does this happen, and what does it mean? Perhaps it is human nature to abandon one's opinions in order to appear in support of the majority, or maybe a few bullies got together and figured out how to manipulate the rest of Congress. Nonetheless, if a politician wants to get any legislation passed on Capitol Hill, they must first follow the crowds and go with the flow. In this way, the representative can establish their reputation and secure their roots in office before they can hope to have enough "weight" in writing and passing laws. The more time that they spend in any political office, the more weight they have in the form of connections, supporters, "friends", and insider information. If this stress was not enough to make a Congressman squirm, they are also regularly lobbied and manipulated by PACs. Money talks, and it is often in the form of legislation that it reveals its intentions.

It is, therefore, easy to see why most politicians who want to make a change attempt to stay in Congress for as long as possible. Then, it's almost as if the power of their incumbency starts getting to their heads. There's the salary, the complete alienation from the "real world," the incredible perks, and months of vacation. PAC bonuses help fill those vacations with exotic luxury.

102

Most people would not turn down this kind of lifestyle, and would certainly fight to get reelected - doing anything possible to stay in office.

You can see this phenomenon first-hand by observing our country's politicians in the news, and their behavior around elections. What is more appalling is their conduct in the House and Senate floor. You may remember learning about "rider bills" in school. A bill being presented to a vote in Congress may be so densely packed with ulterior motives and add-ons that one quickly forgets what the original intent of the law should have been. What's worse is that most Representatives and Senators who are actually present for the voting process have absolutely no idea what the bill is about.

They don't know the contents of the hundreds of pages of this legislation (or most any other) and have no idea as to who wrote it. Why should they waste their time doing the reading when their party has already made the voting decision for them? It's a binary code: (You vote with the party), you can sit at the cool kid table for another year; you vote against your party, and you're kicked out of the cafeteria.

This popularity contest is happening in your country as you read this book. As long as we continue to allow politicians to overstay their welcome in office, they will continue to practice this juvenile behavior with absolutely no regard for your welfare or your family's well being. How true are your Congressional representatives to their publicized platform? Have they been honest to your district's constituents? How many bills that are truly beneficial to us have not passed due to the binary decision each Congressman has to make? We can't fire them because they didn't read the bill or because they voted along their party line, or can we?

This profound lack of honesty and productivity affects each of the 435 members in the House and 100 members of the Senate, and you get 535 members of an unproductive Congress.

# The Binary Party Factor

Let's extend this binary party factor (that vote with their party) to our state governors, city mayors, and councilmen, our selected President, and even the Supreme Court. We have just described our ineffective government and how an honest person becomes a little tainted. Voting for a bill that the Congressperson does not believe in will certainly taint their credibility with the people. The party often forces the Congressperson's hand, but this is hardly an excuse. We can't have senior members of Congress continue running Congress.

> "A long habit of not thinking a thing wrong gives it a superficial appearance of being right."
>
> --Thomas Paine

So the party factor is also a costly and controversial aspect of occupying a Congressional seat. The spending does not end there. Let's take a look at another important ingredient in the political game of getting what we want. Lobbying is the art of influencing decisions of legislators. Lobbying happens in all forms of government. It can be for the good, but when there is significant money involved, it's usually in the best interest of their PAC and a conflict of interest for the public.

Ultimately, if any elected official receives PAC money before or after voting on a bill regarding that industry, a voting line of honesty may have been crossed. This Congressional member is showing the lobbyist that they are here to play the game, and that game is not in the best interest of America. This type of lobbying or contribution of PAC money is done across all party lines. The political affiliation is irrelevant as long as the result is achieved. Until we begin voting smarter, we will continue to be victims of a rigged legal system that affects every aspect of our personal and professional lives. The first step in eliminating this injustice from our country is to become educated of its existence and aware of what is truly going on. When enough people get tired of this blatant infringement on their rights and freedoms, my hope is that they will take to the polls. The next even-numbered November is coming up fast, and with it, perhaps a third of all Senators will be told to pack their things.

## PACs in a Nutshell

With this knowledge in hand, it's easy to feel that the US government is literally bought and paid for. Who are some of these large PAC spenders? They are the oil industry, financial, pharmaceuticals, the defense industry, tobacco, biofuel, mining, telecommunications, the American Medical Association (AMA), insurance companies, and automotive companies, to name a few. The list is long and ugly. It is easy to view who is on the different industry committees. However, it is much more challenging to find the Super PAC contributor names - the very benefactors of that expensive lobbying.

We have the same unknowns with PAC donations right now, with a few billionaires openly donating tens of millions of dollars to some of the presidential campaigns. It is legal for them to accept these donations for running their campaign and paying their campaign staff. The controversial acceptance of PAC campaign contributions and succumbing to lobbyist whims is extremely useful in keeping the same politicians in office as they are already highly polarized to their party line.

One of the reasons that neither party likes Mr. Trump is that he's not a politician and does not owe anyone any favors. What a concept! It is no wonder that the political world doesn't like him - he can't be bought. Treat that last comment as non-partisan, but only if you can find another candidate who, if elected, isn't going to have favors to pay back.

# Chapter Nineteen

## Then There Are Perks

There are laws from which Congressmen are exempt, and consequences are waived. The addictive drug of POWER kicks in (talk about making something illegal - make power illegal – just kidding). It happens to all incumbents, and big money helps keep them in. There are campaign dinners, trips, golf outings, flights and more. According to the research organization Political Money Line, "over the past five years, members of Congress have received more than $18 million to travel the world at the expense of private organizations. These expenditures include 6,242 trips for 628 lawmakers from both political parties."[35]

## Perks and More Perks

1. **Basic earning for Senators and Representatives** - $174,000 per year with the Majority Leader making $193,400 and the speaker of the House making $223,500. **That amounts to over one million dollars per person in six years.**

1. **Health Insurance** – enjoy the lowest rates of any other health care program in the nation.

2. **Retirement** – may be covered by the Civil Service or the Federal Employees program. The number can be as high as 80% of their final salary.

3. **Allowances** – personal staff [18 – 22 members ea.] average per member of Congress is $1,243,560

4. **Expense Allowance** – stationary, business cards, newsletters, domestic travel and lodging, communication expenses.

5. **Franking Privilege** – cost Americans around $50 million a year as it allows senators to send flyers postage free.[36]

6. **Foreign Travel** – includes free use of military aircraft.

Sounds like an excellent program to get involved in. Can I get your support? Write me in for U.S. Senator, House Representative or State Governor. I can imagine how the other 534 Congressmen would react to my "Six Years and Out" agenda.

Here's a question that has gone unanswered - why did the PACs, spend over $20 million dollars to help John Boehner get re-elected in 2014[37]? It's only a two-year term so why pay $20 million to get a representative re-elected for two years? Do they know something that we don't? The guy retired one year later in 2015, so his total funding amounted to about $50,000 a day while he was in office! Ironically, it took a while to find a replacement! Now it will be interesting to see how much money is donated in 2016 to keep the new House leader Paul Ryan in office. His term expires in November of 2016. He will have been in office for 18 years as of the 2016 elections, so he is on the enclosed list of whom not to vote for.

For the Paul Ryan fans out there, we can still implement the "Ten Years Out of Office" rule and reelect him in 2026. By then, he would only be 56 years old, which is around the average age for a Congressperson anyhow. It will also be interesting to see if America's debt will go up or down in those ten years. When Ryan was first sworn into office in 1998 the United States debt was $5 trillion dollars; at the time of writing it's over $19 trillion dollars. The US debt problem cannot be blamed squarely on any one person, but we can certainly track the rise of debt based on specific legislation. Positions of power should, at least occasionally, be used for good not for evil. In the case of Paul Ryan, perhaps he can realize his proposal to cut $5.1 trillion dollars in spending from the US budget now that he's Speaker of the House.[38]

In that time same time frame, there have been nine "different" Congresses, and none of them got the Federal Budget in order. This is not a particularly good indicator of any incumbent's ability to reduce the

National Debt. Holding political office for two years or over six years does not guarantee any changes in policy. This harmful legislation is just a symptom of the core illness – the politician who voted "yay."

Sometimes when the Legislative Branch claims that we have a new Congress, people actually believe that to be true. This deceit can be likened to buying a car. If you purchase a 1998 model in 2016, it may be "new" to you, but it is not new at all. The miles and the wear and tear of overuse are still there. New tires and an oil change cannot make this vehicle new.

The Congressional Research Service notes that the current average age for Representatives of the House is 57, while for Senators it is 62 years old. Although we are looking for non-career politicians, this does not imply that our future candidates will lack in education or experience. The minimum age for entry into office is spelled out in the Constitution, while surely the average age of Senators and Representatives is not expected to waver dramatically.

Our ultimate goal would be only to vote for non-career politicians - ultimately just public servants; ones that promise to respect six years and out. Our definition of "candidate" for public office must not include the word "incumbent." Currently, Congress provides us with just the opposite environment, giving us incumbents but no true candidates. Do you really think our forefathers thought that could ever be a good idea? Of course, not! By gradually changing members, class rotations would prevent senators from permanently combining for "sinister purposes," protect the Senate from rapid idea turnover, and encourage senators to deliberate on measures over time.[39]

It's the belief of many Americans that a "*limited period*" in office would alter the legislative voting behavior. I certainly hope so, and I believe that many of you would agree! Incumbents vote for their own interests; public servants vote for the benefit of the people.

## Incumbents are Expensive

The last three presidents racked up taxpayer debt by staying for a second term. Media Matters and other fact checkers have calculated that George W. Bush has spent almost $20 million just on flights to his Texas ranch.

However, Obama would not be outdone by any Republican. The President and his family went wild spending over $40 million dollars on vacations[40]. To put things in perspective, $40 million dollars spent over the course of 4 years amounts to over $750,000 a month for one family. Now do the words, "American Royalty" have a little more meaning? So where was Congress when all this was happening? If this is something that you want to change, please do so this every election season with your vote.

James Madison, a political theorist and the fourth President of the United States had co-authored a series of papers labeled the "Federalists." He used the words democracy and republic almost synonymously, defining the later as

*"… a government which derives all its powers directly or indirectly from the great body of the people, and is administered by persons holding their offices during pleasure, for a limited period, or during good behavior.*[41]

# Chapter Twenty

## Problems with Career Politicians

After asking questions and listening to comments about replacing Congress we are more aware than ever of the existent problems with career politicians. Most of this country now agrees that we have a reactive Congress, along with legislators that are not controlled by the people. When we allow ourselves to take a step back and look at the big picture, we see that as a voter and citizen, we have no control over anything that is going on in the government. There is no control over the two parties consistently opposing each other in Congress, and no control over their affiliation with PACs, contributors, and big industry lobbyists. The only thing we do have control over is our vote – and guess what, they're trying to take away that control as well by putting limitations and restrictions on our voting freedom.

The conflict between the two sides is not what's hidden behind closed doors; indeed, the conflicts are well-known public assaults on one another – verbally, and politically. Campaigners are great at whistleblowing when they perceive it as a benefit to keeping someone from being elected, but fail to check each other or do any whistleblowing while in office.

Each side is holding ground for their party as though it were a monarchy. This manner of thinking does not only lack in creativity, but it also focuses less on policy and leadership. It is more about catering to their constituents that are truly unknown to us. Or we may think we know who their constituents are – maybe big money lobbyists that get them re-elected. One thing is certain – this style of thinking and lack of leadership in Congress has and continues putting America in the face of danger.

Who are "they" that control our leaders, our economy, our social environment, and our very culture?

110

They have kept thirty-six of our senators in office for more than 30 years! Thirty-four states can start changing who's in the Senate while all fifty states can start to work by changing our House of Representatives.

## How Long Has The United States Had A Congress?

America is currently suffering the effects of our 114th Congress. To calculate the number of years that 114 Congresses have been in session, we take the number of out existing Congress, say the 115th and multiply it by two. The result would show that we have had a Congress for 230 years.

Logic follows that if every two years, we are accounting for a new Congress, we must actually create a new Congress by electing new officials. Remember, every two years one-third of the Senators' terms expire. So by design, replacing Senators one class at a time would mean that all three Classes, I, II, and III or 100 Senators would be replaced every six years.

Each state has two Senators with terms that expire in different years. The two classes were determined by a strategy that allowed for the three classes of Senators to remain as close as possible to the same in size or number.[39] There are 16 or 17 states that only vote for one senator, and therefore do not have the privilege of voting for a new senator every two years as they must wait for the particular Class elections to come around. During those years, these states only get one vote, and that's for their district's House Representative. See the simple voting guideline at the end of the book.

If we begin to use the mantra of "Six Years and Out," today, we would see a complete change of Congress every six years. While four years seems like a long time to wait for change, the alternative is keeping the same lame duck Congress in power.

Doing nothing but hoping that Congress will start to figure it out as a new portion of each class is being replaced every two years. The choice is yours! Maybe our education system will even start to incorporate more material with regard to our Ten Amendments and the Bill of Rights before the next midterm elections. When we go to the voting booth during midterm and presidential elections, how often do we vote out Senate incumbents? That never happens because the odds are not in our favor.

One reason is if a Senator leaves before the end of his or her term a new Senator is appointed by their States governor. So with a little research, you may be able to find which party the Governor belonged to and which party the Senator they chose belongs to. Do you think they would belong to the same party? To make this work each member that served six years or longer must be replaced regardless of the party or their popularity; we thank them and move forward with our next batch of leadership. Remember, most of us until now didn't even know anything about a Senate or Congressional term-limits.

## A Couple of Party Jokes

The idea that any particular party is more conservative or liberal than the other is really only beneficial for conversational labeling and not for voting. It works pretty well in stand-up comedy. Let's give it a try. *When was the last time you knew a conservative that didn't apply for social security or refused Medicare?* The answer: never. Or, *remember the last time liberals controlled Congress, and said hey, stop recording all those phone calls?* The answer: never. Well, *there was that time when it was illegal, when this president called Richard Nixon...,* Funny, it was unlawful then, but it isn't now; when did that law change? Better yet, when is that recording feature going to be on our smart phones so we can record them?

112

We need it for quality assurance and training purposes as well.

Why is PAC money brought up so much in this book? Because they are publically pillaging Americans until we are either all broke or they, get us into another conflict or war. The argument that at least one good politician must be currently holding office would only show an unclear or misunderstanding of the problem. I am sure there are plenty; that's not the problem. The problem is the misuse of the system, which is when 535 legislators are in office for an unlimited amount of time. Look at the last 150 to 240 years of any government. They also did not have term limits. Now they have control over their people and the voting system. If one wants to see a change in any country, the change must come from within – in this case, literally changing the legislative body. It's not quite as simple as choosing one new candidate when 334 are up for re-election. We have to think about changing the entire Congress one-third of them at a time. We have to really need to watch which voting ticket we receive when we go to vote.

If it doesn't have an alternative to the incumbent on it, that ticket isn't any good. We need to get the word incumbent replaced by the words "expired term," and "open seat" - a request I make of both the Senate and House of Representatives. Incumbents will be classified as ineligible for any open positions for a minimum of ten years. If we start thinking that way before we go to the voting booth, it will make it much easier to happen. Only then will America truly have a new Congress.

We can keep saying we have the best government in the world, however, could we honestly say that before 1920? Doing the math, it took our great government over 130 years to get an Amendment passed that allowed Women to vote. Do you think there may be anything else you would like to occur as another 100 years have passed? Keeping our best government in the world is our plan. Just not doing it with long-term politicians in power.

That is like actively molding our government for tyrannical, undemocratic rule.

Much of our existing legislation (federal laws) begs to be revisited, and much of it should be rewritten or repealed. Once again after reviewing several Constitutions from other countries that are lengthy and convoluted documents that appear to be for the people, however, they have exceptions giving control back to the government. America has thousands of unknown statutes a number so large it couldn't even be found. Then there are the 13,000 plus Executive Orders plus there are dozens of federal agency laws we don't know what they're about.

Ralph Waldo Emerson made a profound statement to define success; he wrote, " *...to find the best in others; to leave the world a bit better; to know even one life has breathed easier because you have lived and to laugh often and much; this is to have succeeded.* "

Let's find the "best" in federal laws, eliminate the worst so we know that one more life can breathe easier. Who knows it may affect you and someone you care about profoundly. I have had several people tell me that they would gladly do this for their grandchildren.

# Chapter Twenty-One

## The New Congress

*"We cannot wait for great visions from great people, for they are in short supply. It is up to us to light our own small fires in the darkness."*

-- Charles Handy

Why can't we let Congress create its own term limits? Wouldn't it be something if they had to make a livelihood out of what they have allowed to befall America?  First, their job would be moved out of America because outsourcing jobs cuts costs; Second, the company would likely be acquired by another company called Romney Inc. that eliminated the 535 jobs that demand a salary of $174,000 a year jobs. But then the company would be sold eliminating another 200,000 jobs; Third, benefits and or salary are reduced by 20% while the required labor hours remain the same. Fourth, their support staff would be replaced with customer service from another country whose native language is most certainly not English; Fifth, 30% of their jobs would be replaced by illegal immigrants for 25% less pay and no benefits. And finally, sixth; the company begins to show some of the highest returned earnings in twenty years. Oh, and if they made their own term limits, they would limit them to four terms or only 24 years in office. That would come with a contingency that they could stay in another three terms for good behavior. Any of this sound like a reason to get a new Congress?

## Which Party Controlled Congress When They Voted For Pay Raises?

The last Amendment Congress passed was the 27th. It gave them an automatic pay raise after November elections.

115

That gave them exemption from some laws the rest of us have; a better healthcare system than they created; lifetime entitlements. In fact, existing lifetime benefits need to be repealed. Where is the Conservative party when all this was voted into law? Wait, maybe it was a liberal Congress, and there hasn't been a different Congress since 1964 that has had the thought of rescinding any of this! Just trying to keep this as nonpartisan as possible. These are a few reasons we can't let our Congress create their own term-limits or approve any more Amendment.

## Yea And Nay Voting Goes Twenty-First Century

The current yea and nay, or hand voting, is too influential [Article I Section 5].

You read that right - Congress is still voting based on a show of hands or verbal yea and nay voting. Really! Maybe a New Congress would see the distinct advantage that technology not only can keep track of 1 billion people that it could easily replace this arcane practice. Currently, many members of Congress were in office before smartphones were introduced to the mainstream public. We would all like to believe we think individually – yet there is a certain amount of second-hand influence stemming from the way others are voting as well. Electronic voting with the individual mechanical backup voting system has the advantage of accuracy, speed, and the ability to manually double-check if a recount is in order. We could also check to see how everyone voted 75 years from now.

## National Advertising of Voting Comes Out the Next Day

National advertising of election results needs to be revisited so that states in other time zones are not affected by the outcome of other votes. Influence of media should also be prohibited on election days.

116

Some might even argue that following these guidelines is a matter of national security. It is curious to note that the NSA does not have any qualms about allowing the media to advertise up to the days prior to elections. Currently, each party is taking advantage of the lack of regulation of the media with regard to elections. Sure, the polls make for great media drama, but it would be just as dramatic if the news were to reveal the results the next day, not the night of the elections. People could then watch and discuss every excruciating detail after each time zone has voted – just like Monday night football. Currently, we are but one step away from being able to count each district's votes in every state. If you think that it's acceptable for lobbyists to give massive donations that impact how our legislators vote and you agree with the laws that our selected officials make even though they impact our fundamental rights, then you don't want a new Congress.

There's an old story about a blind man heading towards a well. Another man is standing there and watching him. If the blind man falls into the well, who's fault is it? Does the fault lie with the blind man for not seeing the danger, or with the man who is watching the disaster unfold? Knowing that you could make a difference by doing nothing is just as bad as committing the crime directly. It's a passive aggressive, non-partisan approach, but it is just as impactful as casting a vote for an incumbent.

# Chapter Twenty-Two

## Who Will Take The Place of Career Politicians?

The Booz Allen Hamilton Report of 2010 concluded that being successful in executing strategies for positive change in government is within the control of incoming public leaders.[42]

Imagine that we succeed in dethroning career politicians from Congress. (Let's take a moment to enjoy that thought.) Now, who will fill their seats? Ideally, many of you will agree that we want to be represented by honest, loyal, and intelligent individuals – ones with a practiced common sense that can publically proclaim that they will not be bought. The ideal replacement will have a firm grasp of the simple concepts of finance, that we just cannot spend more money than we make, and that borrowing must be done responsibly and only on a limited basis. We need "elected" legislation that will have a plan on how our debt will be repaid. What's easier? Vote them out or call your Representative and ask what their plan is to pay back this debt? I hope that you're thinking that voting them out is easier. Debt should be at the top of the to-do list for our new Speaker of the House. The bottom line is that we want politicians to have traits of accountability, integrity, and responsibility. It's not that our elected officials didn't have those traits when they took office; it's that our current system of Congress could morph anyone including the Hulk into the type of machine that Congress wants its members to be.

One morning, like many others, I happened upon an individual who had voluntarily shared their opinion of Congress – an occurrence that happens to me rather often than not! It was the first time I have ever met this person, and his opinions were adamant and curt. "They all need to go," he said, in a tone that denoted how obvious his conclusion should be for the greater good of the public. So, I asked the most obvious question in response – "How would you go about doing that?"

The following was the most interesting moment of the conversation as he began to think out loud; "Well, the Constitution would get in the way, wouldn't it?" It's this misconception that leads people to feel that they have no choice or that their vote doesn't matter! Naturally, my response was "No, actually the Constitution was planned exactly for that purpose." I then asked if he knew that we could vote out one-third of the Senate every two years. "Well," he says, "Wouldn't the parties find a way to prevent that?" Many of us voters would come to the same conclusions as this gentleman. His words continuously remind me of why we all need to think outside of the party lines. Although there are a wealth of intell gent people who have something good to offer this country, the sad truth is that newcomers are not only unwelcome in Congress, but are often politically and otherwise attacked in an effort to control, manipulate, and expel them from their post. As we elect new representatives to replace each class of the Senate every two years, that kind of manipulating would ultimately come to an end.

## Anyone a Politician Would Hate

The guidelines for eligibility for Congress are Constitutionally in place - and for most people supplying a birth certificate and proof of residency in their state should be relatively straightforward. Leave the rest up to the voters. Let the media ask the new candidates their questions so that we may dispel any doubt, and fill in the gaps. There is no need to interview outgoing incumbents as they are voted out of legislation. If they want to do something good for America, they can hold a class on their experience. I mentioned earlier that candidates are labeled Conservative or Liberal for purposes of an election. However, this should not be the reasoning used in choosing one candidate over another. I know what you're thinking, "Of course it matters!"

If you're a Republican, you might say that the Liberals want bigger government and sponsorship from the dollars of the upper class. If you're a Democrat, you might say Conservatives are out for themselves and that they don't care about the middle class, just about big money. What we actually need is someone that politicians would hate; someone who gives you a direct answer to a question rather than confusing rhetoric that is impossible to verify. The bigger concern is that ex-politicians are always vying for re-election, and they are our only choice due to a lack of new candidates. This will be a problem until we use our votes to turn over career politicians every two years.

Each party portrays its platform differently. However, when it comes time for campaigning, distinguishing between the parties is nearly impossible. Each week, the candidates change their tune to fit their perception of what the public wants to hear. Here is a list of party definitions, purely for informative purposes at this time.

**1. *Republican*** – Envision a stronger and freer America, the American Dream is one of equal opportunity for all.

**2. *Democrat*** – Believe that we're greater together than we are on our own; that this country succeeds when everyone gets a fair shot, everyone does their fair share, and everyone plays by the same rules.

**3. *Socialist*** – Concerned with caring for the whole or greater number of people through sharing what each has with the others so that all are in good (enough) shape. Organized for the common good.

**4. *Progressive*** – [Not an active party – yet] The dismantling of monopolistic corporations, equitable taxation of businesses, the right to collective bargaining, state ownership of public utilities, public control and protection of the country's natural resources, and an end to fraud and corruption in public offices. Advocating progress, change, improvement, or reform toward better conditions.

**5.** *Whig* - Value differences of opinion and independent thought; do not necessarily take a position on every particular issue that may be fashionable for the moment. Instead, they propose a program of broad reforms that we believe will strengthen our country as it faces the challenges of the 21st century.

**6.** *Centrist* - Centrists don't have party lines. Centrists believe that solutions are more important than biases. Centrism is a political ideology based on reason and pragmatism, considerate of short and long-term thinking. Centrism is not defined by compromise or moderation - it is considerate of them.[43]

## We Can Do Better Than The Electoral College

A quick review of history reveals the probability of how the Electoral College will vote. If a Republican served two terms, the next president would be a Democrat. The same pattern follows if a two-term president were a Democrat; the next president would likely be a Republican. If one is unhappy with the president in the first four years (or be it a state senator, representative, or a governor), doesn't it make sense not to vote them back into office? I have to believe that voters can do better than the Electoral College when it comes to voting for a Congress. History can also teach us that corruption and power are often directly correlated with length of time someone is in office.

Nonetheless, incumbents historically have a huge advantage to outsider candidates because incumbents have the opportunity to make promises to help PAC's; this mainly gets them voted in for another term. It's also well known that big money is continually being donated to keep the "Good Ole Boy" in office and not take a chance of bringing in someone that may not vote in his or her best interest.

We want individuals that make promises to the people and "if" they get elected will leave office after six years.

I.E. During a trip to South Korea, an open microphone recorded President Obama discussing the issue of missile defense with Russian President Dmitri Medvedev. "On all these issues, but particularly missile defense, this can be solved, but it's important for him to give me space," Obama explained, referring to Medvedev. "After my election, I have more flexibility."[44]

These comments reinforce what many of us already know – politicians tells us what we want to hear in order to win our votes, and then go back to their special interest agendas when they are in the clear.

What does the President do in their second term anyhow? While the first term is occupied with implementing new policies, the second term seems to be traditionally relegated to campaigning for the president's political party, the occasional presidential pardon, and possibly choosing another Supreme Court Justice. In short, the second term seems rather unproductive, and therefore its necessity is questionable.

Bringing in a one-third new Congress would certainly keep a president busy in the second term. In two more years, another one-third will be voted in, and we will have a majority representation of new ideas in Congress.

If an idea is good and it's good for the American people, should it matter which party brought the idea to Congress? The correct answer is no. Implementing terms limits is a policy that will allow us to introduce new ideas, establish faster resolution of legislation, reduce the size of government, diminish national debt, and improve our budgeting ability all while creating jobs in America.

*"Never give in. Never give in. Never, never, never, never - in nothing, great or small, large or petty - never give in, except to convictions of honor and good sense. Never yield to force. Never yield to the apparently overwhelming might of the enemy."*                    *--Winston Churchill- -*

## Remembering Freedom

Those readers who are under the age of 45 don't even remember the freedoms that America has lost in the last twenty years. Strikingly, even a larger readership demographic is not aware that churches lost a major portion of their First Amendment in 1954 when Lyndon Johnson successfully passed an amendment that prohibited churches and tax-exempt organizations from participating in politics by endorsing or opposing candidates. Some speculate that politically motivated church gatherings were a threat to Johnson's re-election to a second term as president.

In 1951, Congress ratified the 22nd Amendment, which ensured that no president was to serve more than two terms in his lifetime. It's not a Constitutional requirement for senators or representatives to be elected again. However, it is quite clear that they shall vacate upon expiration of their Class. It is also evident that Representatives shall be chosen every second year. These interpretations are presented with a factual understanding that the words, "shall vacate" mean they will leave office. It is our hope that this right will always be up to the people to enforce. Is November of 2016 a good time to start? This quote about Congress is important enough to hear a second time.

*"Is there anyone out there in the world, real world, that believes that what's going on in the Congress of the United States is good? Our approval rating is lower than North Korea's."*

*--Harry Reid, July 14, 2013*[45]

*"The new source of power is not money in the hands of a few, but information in the hands of many."*

*--John Naisbitt*

## What Does Your Vote Cost?

*How To Replace Congress* emphasizes the idea of focusing voting decisions back onto The People, and reducing some of the over-fixation of siding with a particular party's ideology.  The parties currently do enough advertising for themselves at monumental costs, with the average campaign costing around ten million dollars per senator. It can be easily speculated that contributions such as this make it much more appealing for incumbents to remain in office for longer than six years. **The money spent to re-elect senators translates not only into fiscal cost, but also a tariff on our freedom.** Someone else is stealing those votes right out from under our noses by buying us out. Super PACs want to control how each legislator makes decisions. The freedom tariff translates into lost jobs, higher telecommunication cost, loss of infrastructure in America, loss of individual freedoms, higher fuel cost and higher health-care cost to name a few.

PACs cover their bases, and they don't care which party is in office as long as the legislator is helping them out. We should take a hint from PACs and adjust our attitude to reflect that it doesn't matter which party is in office as long as Congress is helping America.

Now you don't have to believe what you are reading here, but all the information is open to the public. OpenSecrets.org is one website that I recommend for finding unbiased information regarding money in politics, lobbyist data, and analysis.

The point is that the above I-don't-want-to-believe-it-to-be-true information about the individual that you voted for is not the source of the problem at hand; the source of the problem is always the other party. See how this works? Just blame the other side! The other party has you believing that the bad guys are on the other side of the line.

## Who Are the Bad Guys?

Here is the reality of it – get ready for this –the bad guys are our Congress as a whole.  Does corruption begin before or after elections? Corruption can take seed at any point in the process. Before an election, corruption takes the form of PAC money funding a campaign. In the aftermath, corruption rears its ugly head in the form of legislature and voting actions that support the PACs that have poured money into the incumbent's campaign.

Article I Section I of the Constitution states, "all legislative powers herein granted shall be vested in a Congress of the United States…" Well, it feels like the government is running us, not the other way around. The word "vested" also means to entrust power - it doesn't say to abuse it. Let's not forget the repeated abuse of power that's occurring in our own federal agencies. We have some idea of misuse, though doubtfully the entire picture of the disturbing mismanagement of programs like We fare, Social Security, and now the National Healthcare program. All governmental programs have cost. Sometimes they are positive and sometimes negative. The above-mentioned programs are needed and should not be abused.

## How Politicians Become Corrupt And How We Pay For It

In May of 2013, an article in the Boston Globe gave us a small glimpse of the daily lives of our Congressmen. As it were, newly elected officials, or "freshmen," are instructed by their party affiliates to reserve four hours of each day in order to raise funds.[46]

The Huffington Post attests to this news, elaborating on the PowerPoint presentation given by party leaders urging their Freshman members to spend as much as four hours a day making fund-raising calls. This practice is not limited to just one party but is a common approach for newly elected officials of all parties.[47]

Perhaps most new Congressmen enter into their first term bright-eyed and ready to make a true difference in the lives of their constituents. However, they are quickly sucked into the established modus operandi of Capitol Hill – that is, if you want to check off any items on your political agenda, you better start paying it forward to the party bosses and pull your weight.

This book is not the first written disclosure of the secrets on Capitol Hill. Nonetheless, we voters prefer to close our eyes to the depravity in government and continue to vote for incumbents or abstain from voting entirely. The question is, "why"? An intellectual study out of Claremont Graduate University explains that toxic leaders have a special knack for fulfilling people's deep-rooted psychological needs. Toxic leaders promise a utopia that provides for our need of security and authority. They know how to make us feel special, and feed to that desire to belong. They promise to protect us from being ostracized and feeling powerless – but in order to do this, they typically choose another group of people to use as scapegoats and to label as "the enemy" that is creating all these problems.

126

Perhaps more worrisome is this revelation by Dr.Jean Lipman-Blumen, the author of the article;

*Given the strong need for leaders, followers who are confronted with toxic leaders unsurprisingly find excuses to tolerate them. Employees submit to bad bosses because they want their paychecks or are afraid to be left jobless. People think they incur a personal risk if they confront a toxic leader, due to their need for order or their fear that a new boss could be worse.* [48]

This behavior of tolerance for fear of something worse directly echoes our behavior as voters and citizens. We complain about our current leadership, but have resigned ourselves to the current situation, thinking that nothing can change for the better.

## Our Weapons Investment Division

Ciponline.org is the web platform for a think tank and research group dedicated to providing information and transparency concerning corruption, war, inequality, and climate change. The Center for International Policy provides many details on how the weapons industry "donates" money to America's legislation. They track the illicit arms sales that pass through the hands of the government Armed Service Committee, Strategic Forces Subcommittee, and other legislative sponsors promoting the purchase of weapons for war and armed conflicts. In this case, one might argue that the government is putting the Second Amendment at risk by participating in the aforementioned activities. Just a reminder, without donations, a political incumbent, ceases to exist.

*"Freedom is the last, best hope of earth."*         --Abraham Lincoln--

# Chapter Twenty-Three

## Is Our Government Becoming Its Parent?

America's government was structured wonderfully with the concept of having checks and balances. These measures have long been abused and even outright ignored. Our legislators seem to live above the laws that they issue. It's time for them to get checked and for balance to be restored. **They are in our house [America] not theirs [the government], they need to respect our Rights** and not continue to limit those Rights or to control us.

Is our government turning into its own parent? Did Congress rebel and leave the house [Great Britain] in 1776, then come back to their senses around the 1890's and decide its parent **[the King]** had the right idea about how a country should be run – with one person or a small group of individuals making biased decisions for everyone else?

In an interesting play on roles, let's take a look at our Declaration of Independence of 1776 and replace references to the oppressive King with the word "Congress" (our current Congresses):

*He* **[Congress]** *has refused his [its] Assent to Laws, the most wholesome and necessary for the public good. He* **[Congress]** *has refused for a long time, after such dissolutions, to cause others to be elected,* **[our voting is limited to a specific party]** *whereby the Legislative Powers, He* **[Congress]** *has erected a multitude of New Offices, and sent hither swarms of Officers to harass our people and eat out their substance.* **[the agencies are listed throughout the book]** *He* **[Congress]** *has kept among us, in times of peace, Standing Armies without the Consent of our legislatures.* **[to open all our mail and record all our electronic communication]** *He* **[Congress]** *has combined with*

128

*others to subject us to a jurisdiction foreign to our Constitution, and*

*unacknowledged by our laws; giving ~~his~~ Assent to their Acts of pretended*

*Legislation:* **[laws that break the First Amendment]**

*For imposing Taxes on us without our Consent:* **[19 Trillion in debt]**
There's a reason Congress has such a poor rating.

It would appear that we would like the same Independence today for what the United States fought for from 1776 to 1811. Instead of having a Declaration of War we can have a Declaration of a voting Revolution. Instead of fighting against an Army from Great Britain with weapons and daily carnage of war, every two years we line up at the voting booth armed with knowledge not weapons that Patriots will not be voting for incumbents as positive change in how we are being governed is what we really want.  t will be the Loyalist that does not want to bring morality back into our government and are still weak from being compelled to vote along a specific party line.

# Chapter Twenty-Four

## What About the House Representatives?

*"A leader must identify himself with the group, must back up the group, even at the risk of displeasing superiors."*

*-- Vince Lombardi*

Term limits are applicable for Representatives of the House as well as Senators. For decades, we have seen House Representatives displeasing the people by following House Leaders; this is not in the best interest of America. For Representatives, the importance of our voting power comes into play. It is well known that ambitious Congressmen have stayed in office for several decades. We need this message to get out to as many people as possible for one-third of all Representatives to be replaced at least every six years.

From a political perspective, Congress has structured itself to keep those incumbents in office. For the parties, it's a game of control and the pawns are the Representatives themselves. The party that wins is the one that has more representatives in office, and therefore more votes to support their interests. The legislators who flex the rules by redrawing district lines in order to keep their Representatives in office are the same ones that create our taxes and determine the federal budget. PACs contribute millions of dollars to keep particular representatives in office for longer than two years, such as in the case of Speaker of the House John Boehner, who received over $20 million dollars for his 2014 campaign. Raising this awesome amount of money did not stop Boehner from retiring just a year later. His one-year term cost over $50,000 per day in PAC contributions.

What is important to understand is all this campaigning, the drawing of district lines and or PAC contributions are not in the Constitution. So are any of these newly written laws illegal? Just because Congress writes a law that favors legislators does not make it Constitutional. Even newly passed state laws that are not necessarily constitutional. The fact that these laws are enforceable is a great injustice on the part of our people. However, the situation is not impossible to resolve. We can still repeal these laws with legislators who are truly on our side – newly elected public servants who are not corrupted by their long tenure in any political office.

The fixed voting system has been created slowly over the last 100 years by a government that wants to have control over the people. People did not create this, but we have allowed it to happen. If people had known about how voting in one-third of Congress would be in their favor, we would have had 17 entirely new Congresses in within a single century. We can't change the past, but we can plan for our future!

The simplest way to move forward is by using a "Six Years & Out" voting process. Limiting individuals to that length of time in office would all but eliminate unneeded political practices. Regardless of party affiliations, by electing officials one-third of Congress at a time they would be representing the people.

## Changing of the Guard

Campaigning requires a tremendous amount of money and a great deal of time and energy. Instead of campaigning, our legislators could be passing laws that benefit the people, rescinding laws that have taken away our rights, and reducing the size of government. Our Congress has the potential to make or break America. They are the guards of our country and its time for *"the changing of the guard."*

The idea of voting in a whole new Congress is not a new concept.

Rotating one-third of our Senators every two years was always considered a method of protecting the people from a government that desired more power. The government, however, has not only figured out a way to stay in office they also figured out a way to do it while accepting massive amounts of money. We need to show them why the words, "chosen every second year," were written in the Constitution.

The House of Representatives has also shown us that six years has been too long to be in office. The pull to use their official power for personal gain appears to grow as they fully realize their potential after some time in office. The Washington Post fact checkers found that over two dozen members of Congress have been indicted since 1980.[49] Perhaps it was their incredible foresight that drove our forefathers to limit representatives to a two-year term.. It's logical to conclude that they knew more about how the government could amass an excess of power if officials were allowed to remain in office for too long. Those powers are in the Declaration of Independence and have been pointed out to be somewhat similar to today's problems with our modern government. Here is one example - *"He has erected a multitude of new offices, and sent hither swarms of officers to harass our people, and eat out their substance."* Does this sound anything like the dozens of agencies that currently exist in the United States?

The 1776 Declaration of Independence is as valid today as it was then. This very comprehensive one-page document is the reason for the creation and perpetuation of our Bill of Rights.

# When Did Your Representative Tell You About Receiving PAC Money?

We currently don't like elected officials campaigning while in office, but can't legally stop them from doing so unless we change the way we vote. We have enough of that going on with our presidents when they spend time campaigning to get elected for a second term. Why is so much PAC money being spent in the second term to keep the incumbent in office? Does anyone remember their Representative bringing the millions of dollars back to their constituents and making a promise to use the money for good, not evil? Second terms have historically garnered billions of dollars, yet their recipients have far from given us the bang for the buck that we deserve – regarding legislation that is created to uphold our rights and preserve our freedoms.

I hope the message is clear that our government's current algorithm or the way they attempt to solve problems won't change anytime soon unless we have a paradigm shift in our voting practices.

## The Here and The Now

Our current and past Commander in Chiefs and their families enjoy taxpayer-supported vacations, entertainment, and foreign travel, along with other perks that only a family of royalty could afford.

Why would the President, or any Congressman who is enjoying similar benefits want to purposely change their lifestyle if he or she can find ways to stay in office? Congressmen are supposed to be the whistleblowers on out of control spending or the writing of Executive Orders that have an adverse impact on our rights. They don't blow the whistle because they are enjoying many of those same benefits.

Here's the who, what, where, when, why, how, and "easy" of changing how Congress is run now and in the near future:

1) **The Who:** Listed in the appendix or you can look them up yourself

2) **The What:** Voting The People's Term Limits of "Six Years & Out."

3) **The Where:** Is casting your vote behind that curtain of truth

4) **The When:** November midterm and presidential elections

5) **The Why:** If we care about corruption we must act now

6) **The How:** Is simple; it's how we vote

7) **The Easy:** The lowest rated Congress in United States history

One hindering tactic to being voted out of office is the Representatives' ability to regularly change voting districts. Do you know what district number you are in? Did you know that districts are based on the population of not just American citizens, but also non-citizen residents and even illegal immigrants? Take a look at the list of states in the back of this book and the number of representatives in CA, FL, TX, LA, and NY. Is anyone else seeing a different perspective on the impact of illegals from any country living in the United States? These are all border states or states with international airports or even shipping ports.

*xperience teaches us that it is much easier to prevent an enemy from posting hemselves than it is to dislodge them after they have got possession."*

*-- George Washington*

# Chapter Twenty-Five

## We Hope That These Points Were Made Crystal Clear

*1. It is not about which party to vote for.*

*2. It is not about putting the blame on any particular party, legislator, existing law, or president.*

*3. It is about hitting the refresh button [voting] and getting a new Congress every two years.*

Pointing the finger doesn't solve problems. What's done is done, and it's time to move forward. Moving forward means change - and that change takes effort. It's about identifying problems and finding solutions. To implement a change, we must stop repeating an action that we know doesn't work. I am not claiming that this is the answer, but it is an approach to help us understand that it is time for a change. In life, if you bring out an idea, others also come out with additional solutions to solve the problem.

Our government system and the economy have been reduced by the weight of our enormous national debt and our political inadequacy. The Donkeys and Elephants proclaim to be reducing government cost of operation, and they have had well over 100 years to make that happen. The cycle of blaming the other party and talking ceaselessly about the problem has not brought us solutions. There is an endless and overwhelming supply of information on our government; its operation, how it was set up, why it was established, identities of the participants, and duration of their operation. We need to reduce the size of our bureaucracy and increase the effectiveness and accountability of our government.

# Accepting That We Have Problems

Congress knows it has a problem, but people need to agree that we have a problem either with our system of government or within our system of government. Let's call these problems - "Fundamental Problems" or more precisely, "Congress."

Next, let's identify and isolate the symptoms, and focus on what is fundamentally wrong at the core.

## Examples of Fundamental Problems in Congress:

1) Not getting anything done, no progress on decision-making
2) Legislators care too much about politics, not about this country
3) Budget deficit, with out of control spending and borrowing of money
4) Violating Rights of the people and breaking Constitutional laws
5) No accountability, the need for term limits
6) Lack integrity, dishonesty
7) Party gridlock, bickering, not compromising

Notice anything about this list? Each item screams of non-productivity!

### Examples of Real Problems Congress Should Be Resolving:

1) *Protect our Borders*
2) *Helping to grow the economy and create more U.S. jobs*
3) *Immigration reform*
4) *Create a better and more cost-effective education system*
5) *Review and throw out outdated pieces of legislation*
6) *A smaller, cost-effective, more efficient, and accountable, government that protects our borders and national interest*

*Legislation needs to stop breaking Federal Laws [most of our Bill of Rights] and give the rights back to the people of the United States. The Bill of Rights was created to protect the people from their government.*

*Let's add a seventh problem to our "real" list;*

*7). Remove outdated laws that exercise federal force over individual states. A few worth mentioning again are; The Patriotic Act, McCain-Feingold Act, HIPAA, 501-3c, and others like the Cuban Adjustment Act (CAA) of 1966 (P.L. 89-732). Furthermore, we should remove limitations on the ballot that force people to register for specific parties and only vote for that registered party in primaries. If we can get the parties to admit new candidates on the ballot, it would be a small step towards voting out incumbents.*

## More Efficient Does Not Mean Less!

The above seven real problems are a short list and could be expanded on immensely. For the purpose of this read, enumerating these issues should be enough to get the point across that legislators themselves are the biggest problem.

Our 100 Senators and 435 Representatives have shown that it's almost impossible for Republicans and Democrats to agree with each other. The problem is not that with the number of members in Congress, but rather with their stagnant immovability that perpetrates most of our lame duck Congress issues. We need to increase efficiency by replacing what has been inefficient.

# Chapter Twenty-Six

## Freedom is Not Free

History has taught us that freedom, in fact, is not free. It is a greater issue than which party you do or don't belong to. Our government has many resources that it implements to affect our freedom as Americans. The scale and usage of those powers and resources have been unprecedented in our current and past administrations. There have been over 13,000 executive orders in our history. [50]

Executive Orders 11921, 10990, 10995, 11004, and 11005 are on government sites but difficult to find. They appear to have been amended dozens if not hundreds of times. The level of complexity to these documents is illustrated by the impossibility of having one agreed upon interpretation from any given law firm. These combined laws have all the appearances that allow the government's Federal Emergency Preparedness Agency (FEMA) to develop plans for establishing control over the mechanisms of production and distribution of energy sources, wages, salaries, credit, and the flow of money in U.S. financial institutions **during any undefined national emergency.** When the President declares a state of emergency, Congress cannot review the action for six months thereafter. These laws allow for the takeover of all modes of transportation and control of highways and seaports, and to seize and control the communication media. Moreover, the Housing and Finance Authority has the power to relocate and establish new habitation centers for populations, take over railroads, inland waterways, and public storage facilities.

# Do Laws Take Away Our Rights to Protect Our Freedom?

The Declaration of Independence, the Constitution, and the Bill of Rights were created in order to ensure freedom for all citizens of the United States.

The Bill of Rights guarantees individuals certain basic protections as citizens, including freedom of speech, religion, and the press; the right to bear and keep arms; the right to peaceably assemble; protection from unreasonable search and seizure; and the right to a speedy and public trial by an impartial jury.

In war we have enemies, and there is a dreadful cost to fight for our freedom. In peace, we are to be friends, and we should not have to be burdened by our own government to have freedom.


*"If freedom of speech is taken away, then dumb and silent we may be led, like sheep to the slaughter."*

*-- George Washington*


## Maintaining Freedom Is Not Free


How much does freedom really cost? We don't have a calculator big enough to count the zero's. We have armies of federal inspectors and enforcers in the NSA, TSA, ATFE, CIA, FBI, Home Land Security (HDS), FEMA, IRS, OSHA, and others listed in the book. Many or all of these agencies may be needed, but who should give them oversight? You guessed it, Congress.

Congress supervises these agencies and approves their budgets. The sheer scope of this work has overwhelmed our legislators. They can neither manage overlapping agencies nor cope with the downsizing of unnecessary bodies.

Anyone that has been on a Board of Directors knows what I'm talking about. You have to look at and understand the need for each agency, if its objectives are being accomplished and whether it has outlived its usefulness.

## Freedom: The power to think, and act without restraint; The state of not being subject to do an undesirable thing.

If we know our Constitution is the only way to protect ourselves from being abused, we need a Congress that is going to uphold it by using our votes to replace those [the entirety of Congress] that violate it. Congress continues to grasp for more power via hidden bill riders, agencies, and other means. Until we institute true term limits, this will not change. The Constitution should not be used against us, but to strengthen the freedom and rights of the people.

The Health Insurance Portability and Accountability Act of 1996, and the USA PATRIOT Act (instituted to deter and punish terrorist acts in the United States and around the world, to enhance law enforcement investigatory tools, and for other purposes) are just two of the laws that have interfered tremendously in our lives as citizens.

*"Guard against the impostures of pretended patriotism."*

*-- George Washington*

The Patriot Act creates incredible restrictions on our rights as Americans and deteriorates other aspects of our lives – particularly our

140

privacy. This Act allows government agencies to wiretap our phones, read our emails, and conduct surveillance on any person of suspicion. The Patriot Act is a law that was written out of fear and not one out of possibilities.

I am not suggesting there is a better country in the world to live in than America. What I am saying is that our government should not pass legislation or create agencies that take away our rights. The government should find ways to return the rights and freedoms they have taken away from us. Voting is not only about eliminating political corruption, but it's also about getting our Rights and Freedoms back. The only way is by electing vigilant candidates and letting incumbents know that their job is running on low battery. We don't need to recharge them; we need to replace them as they are not rechargeable.

# Chapter Twenty-Seven

## That's Just The Way It Is

In response to our government, some might say, well "that's just the way it is," and it's always been that way. So why worry about it now? Our broken government may be impossible to fix, but it can be replaced before it breaks our country completely. The way Congress fixes something is by writing new laws with penalties for not upholding that law. Using a little common sense could repair a lot of these problems.

The "Six Years and Out" argument is further strengthened by the mere fact that senators spend much of their sixth year in office campaigning, instead of legislating. While campaigning, they continue to receive an annual salary of at least $174,000. Multiply that by the thirty-four presiding senators and you have $5,916,000 in campaign spending plus their staff cost. That amounts to a small fortune! Now take the 435 representatives making the same $174,000 per year, and factor in their campaigning cost every two years as well. Can we truly rely on the words, "That's just the way it is," and allow this absurdity to carry on?

I am not saying that Representatives spend the entire year campaigning because that would be $75,690,000.00 plus staff cost every two years. As you can see, it doesn't take long for this to add up to a lot of wasted tax dollars that go down the drain every two years. To understand the magnitude of this impact over a six-year change of 100 Senators and 435 House of Representatives, taxpayer savings for those six years could amount to $500,000,000, or half a billion dollars.

So let's look at that same scenario if they were working in the private sector and simultaneously trying to find a similar six-figure job.

If their boss was privy to the employees' job search activities, co you believe that she would continue to pay them $174,000 a year? Do you think the employer would rather kick them out? Of course, she would fire them, if they were looking for another job while raking in a six-figure salary for doing nothing!

## It Would Be One Giant Company With 535 Employees With All Of Them Making Over $174,000.00 Per Year

Think of how large a company would have to be that has 469 employees all making $174,000 a year, and all of them looking for a new job every two years. Now, "That's the way it is with our existing incumbents being allowed to be voted back into office." Let's add this up, 435 House of Representative's + 34 Senators x $174,000 = $81,606,000 just in the 2016 elections. While I still have your attention, this all goes away if they can't be re-elected. My calculator broke trying to multiply this over the last 20 years of voting this way. Simple math with inflation says it's over $1,000,000,000 (One Billion Dollars) of taxpayer-supported campaigning. That would be one giant company that had expenses of over $81,000,000 every two years because their employees were allowed to job hunt. I wonder what that company's revenue is? Better yet, what do they produce that has such a high demand despite its big-ticket price? Maybe Romney Inc. will buy it and outsource everyone.

The next job, should they have the brilliant luck of landing one, would have a 30-hour work week and probably be an LTE, with thirty to eighty percent less pay, and diminished and or no benefits. Now, "That's just the way it is" for the real workforce in America. But what do we do with these non-productive people? We give them a leg up by voting them back into office because they are the incumbents. If this is using our common sense, it has turned into nonsense.

## Hiding the Big Secrets

Corruption in government may be a big seller for the media, as there are many books, movies, and TV shows that, of course, must all be fiction. In actuality, there are a number of books on most topics of political corruption. There have been hundreds of movies produced that are based on real events in politics because political corruption is stranger than fiction. One example of non-fiction is not releasing the 50 plus years of locked up reports on the assassination of President John F. Kennedy. Is there something we can do so that reports like that never get buried again? The answer is yes, and we have one chance every two to four years in starting to make it a reality! Perhaps the documentary *Dark Legacy* on Netflix can put the Kennedy cover-up into a new perspective.

Our elected officials have tried your patience for 50-plus years with this and many other hidden reports, cover-ups, and other political scandals or acts of terrorism. Unsurprisingly our current Congress has nothing to say about their indiscretions. So who does have the authority to bring this information forward? I bring this up because many of us have and continue to vote for the same people - and that methodology isn't working.

I've asked a lot of people if they would ever vote for the opposite party. Surprisingly they say yes. At any rate, most people say that it's difficult to tell one party from the other. Many would say they were not sure which party or candidate lied more often. I know talk is cheap but look at the list from your own state and please note one thing; many of these politicians have been in office for 18 to 42 years, and almost all of them have held office for a minimum of six years. Their legacies account for three terms for over 300 members of Congress.

144

Switching political sides, like going over to the Tea Party, was exactly what Rick Perry did when it suited his political motives. For Reagan, it was a sudden switch to the Republican Party that allowed him to advance and succeed in politics. These two men are examples of career minded politicians who do not let any lines limit their ambitions. If a party line is of so little consequence to them, then why do we continue to vote for the party and not the individual? "That's the way it is." Rick was able to collect wages for being a Texas Governor while at the same time collecting from his retirement program and from social security. Is this how a true conservative responds to social programs? It's setting quite the precedent for other incumbents to follow. I hope you agree that this would be an example of what we don't want to see repeated. Talk about conservative entitlements, wow! Remember Rick's comment, "*It's for the voters to decide*"?

Maybe you have watched or read about the State of the Union Address given by President Obama in February 2014. There was much talk but no real action regarding what some may perceive as a direct threat by a U.S. President. In his own words, he threatened to bypass Congress and run the country through Executive Order. There had to be a few Constitutional violations in that speech. That was an example of when the House of Representatives should have done something and did nothing.

If you have ever had a complaint with a president from either party, remember it's your district representative that you should be complaining to; or maybe stop complaining and vote. Here is the tough part, and the real point of our lame duck Congress. Each branch of our government has sworn an oath and a duty to defend the Constitution.

Rather than unite to defend its institutional prerogatives, the Senate is relying on the Supreme Court to resolve the matter.

If congress does not call the President out when there are alleged violations of the Constitution, shouldn't both branches of Congress also be considered in breach of that sacred sworn oath to the United States? Presidents have been violating the Constitution almost from the inception of America. Notably, the most recent Congresses, (104th through 114th) makes our government look more like an oligarchy where very few people are really ruling this country.

## Selfies and the Fourth Amendment

You may want to read our Fourth Amendment regarding search and seizure violations. I know many of you don't care if they are watching you, "because you don't do anything wrong." That may be so, but do you think it's acceptable for our government and all the individuals who work there to view your personal communications and information? Included in the open book to your life are pictures, letters, documents or anything else you put on the cloud. Many people do not take the necessary precautions to encrypt and secure sensitive personal and work documents before uploading them to a host or sending them via email. This information is not only open to our government but to any person in our country and abroad who can gain access to it. Do you think the United States is the only country in the world looking at your stuff? Once the third party has a hold of your confidential information, they have the power to do with it whatever they wish. As if that idea is not scary enough, just consider how many hackers out there are getting a live-stream of your life. Your phone has a camera, and it can be turned on via remote access, just like your computer. If you don't believe me or the media reports on these occurrences, ask Apple.

What good is a Bill of Rights if it is not being enforced by our civil servants, and is quite pointedly being infringed upon? Our human rights are being violated by the very government that was put in place to protect us. While the US government closely monitors its own people, it has virtually no idea as to how many people are entering our country illegally, and who these individuals are. Government's failure of protecting our borders is what leads them to pass all these infringing laws. They need to deal with who may be in the United States, stop that leak, and send back those that don't belong here.

# Chapter Twenty-Eight

## Six-Year Questions To Gain Perspective

1) **JOBS** - What were you doing six years ago? Did you a have higher paying job, or any job at all? Are you able to spend more of your income or less? Could you retire or are you able to retire now? Did the job market grow to include more full-time jobs or allow us to work more hours for the same pay? Are we able to have more paid free time, more benefits, or the opposite?

2) **ENERGY** - What was the price of fuel six years ago - was it higher or lower? Did electricity, Internet, television, and heating cost increase in proportion to your income? Had it been a healthy, growing economy, the prices should have come down with the surplus, technological advancements, free markets, and the boom in alternative energy. How much higher are costs today than they were six years ago? Did the US get less dependent on fossil fuel or did we drill and ship oil out of the U.S., to other countries, thereby creating more dependence? Did we have liquefied petroleum gas shortages? Check out LP cost six years ago and compare them up to February 2016. Costs were up as high as 600%.[51]

3) **NET-WORTH-** Has our net worth gone up or has it gone down? (Statistics say it is down 40%)[52] Are we able to save money on current income, and if so, earn a higher interest rate? Has home or property value increased or decreased? Did property taxes go down as much as property value has declined? Has the number of bank owned properties increased or decreased? Why?

4) **PROSPERITY** - such as happiness in your job and welfare of family and friends. Has your wealth grown?  Has health care quality and cost become better or worse?

5) **LAWS & LEGISLATION** - Are there more or fewer laws today than six years ago? Are laws hindering economic growth? Are laws reducing our freedoms? Have insurance costs outgrown their worth?

6) **SAFETY & PRIVACY** – For those of you that have the Internet, emai , or cell phones -- is it more or less comforting that the NSA is no: only recording but also storing every phone call, email, and web search that you do?  Does this make you feel any safer knowing that your information is being stored not only by the gove'nment but also by your Internet provider, all because of federal law? When did we vote on this massive government storage concept? What else are they not telling us that isn't a natio1al security issue? *Why do they treat us like terrorists at airports [TSA (Transportation Security Administration) maybe TSA is just a little overpowering]?*

7) **BANKING & INTEREST** – *Do you think that interest rates on CD's will e/er go back up to 10% or as high as 16%? It's very unlikely. With our $20 trillion-dollar debt, the Fed can't afford to raise CD rates for fear that our creditors will raise interest rates on America. By us keeping the same people in office will render the same results.*

# What About WTC 7

Before you start to defend the need for the TSA in our airports, I would urge you do a little bit of an Internet research regarding the 47-story building called WTC 7. That building was also destroyed on 9/11. What's significant about this is that there no aircraft that hit the building, and no other terrorist assault that destroyed it that day, yet it collapsed in a precisely vertical fashion. Nothing hit it! Also look at what was on the 23rd floor of this building and then check to see what day they evacuated that floor and just moved to another location. While you're at it, look at what portion of the Pentagon was hit on 9/11. It was a wing that was more sparsely populated than the rest. How to Replace Congress is not a book about conspiracies but when you can line up that many coincidences in a row, you start to question what really happened. There is such a thing as non-coincidences. There have been multiple national tragedies that lack logical explanations and remain unresolved in the eyes of the people – particularly the families and individuals that are affected. One example is the Oklahoma bombing. It is still unclear why several agents called in sick the day of this horrific event. We continue to mourn the victims of these tragedies, and remember the Sandy Hook shooting and other heartbreaking tragedies that never should have happened - and certainly not in the United States. Legislators seem to be more interested in staying in office and gaining greater control over the citizens of the United States rather than protecting the borders of our country. If one-third of Congress was to be removed, every two years all of the non-national secrets could be made public. Possibly many of these secretive events would then stop happening!

When the Declaration of Independence was first published in 1776, its authors yearned to find a way to share it with as much of the population of America as possible (at the time, it was roughly 2.5 million people). It was Thomas Paine that wrote several pamphlets supporting those efforts.

In his pamphlet series called *"American Crisis,"* Paine wrote, "These are the times that try men's souls." His pamphlets on *Common Sense* echoed the sentiment; "Society in every state is a blessing, but Government, even in its best state, is but a necessary evil; in its worst state an intolerable one: for when we suffer, or are exposed to the same miseries by a Government, which we might expect in a country without Government, our calamity is heightened by reflecting that we furnish the means by which we suffer."

If Congress is to change, we have to provide the means to this change, the same way that we provided the means for the creation of our government in the first place. Simply put, if we want term limits, we need to stop voting for incumbents. I used the above self-evident quotes because it apparently has not been evident to voters. If it were evident, we would have one-third of a new Congress every two years.

If you are tired of political corruption, don't promote it; show Senators that campaigning is no longer an option. Let's show career politicians that incumbent does not mean candidate, that PAC money and returning favors is unacceptable. Show them that we have an oath to uphold. You can take the Pledge of Allegiance out of our schools, but you can't take it out of our hearts. **There are many words that could have been chosen for corruption, but there is only one antonym for it, and it's called honesty.**

# Have We Been Myth-Construed?

**Myth I -** There is too much emphasis on politicians having or needing a legal background.

**Reality** - What we need are honest people who use common sense coupled with a desire to help Congress in a timely manner and to make legislation easier to understand. Unjust laws need to be repealed, un-Constitutional laws rescinded and we don't need lawyers to do either.

**Myth II -** We do not need bills that are voted on before we know what is in the bill.

**Reality** - We need to know the bill's full meaning, and how it will be funded. Each bill must have a single purpose and a requirement before either the House or the Senate can bring a bill to the floor for a vote.

**Myth III -** The party you have aligned with is working towards your best interest.

**Reality -**The party doesn't even know who you are; unless perhaps you have donated $100,000 or more to the incumbent. Have you ever heard of the Majority and Minority House Leaders or Senate Majority and Minority Leaders? The 2014 Speaker of the House had over $20 million dollars donated to his campaign; do you think he remembers who you are? I don't remember him mentioning your names when he quit.

If you have ever donated to a party, you know what I am talking about. They just ask for more and more contributions. The reality is they are already in office. Change takes them out of office. Another striking issue is the number of incumbents' family members who are paid out of their campaign funds. We can put an end to this dishonesty once PAC money is made ineffective.

# Chapter Twenty-Nine

## Making This Dream a Reality

No changes in government will ever happen until there is a complete replacement of Congress. Every complaint that we have ever had, or will have about government leads back to Congress. Not happy with the President today or any President for the last seventy-five years? Look to Congress. The past cannot be undone; we need to get over it. It is about what we can do now. I do not like to use the words "don't," "can't," "never," "won't" or "impossible."

However, if we **"don't"** change the way that we've been voting for over 228 years, we **"can't"** expect a change in our country, or in our lives. The two parties will **"never"** bring us candidates that will go up against their incumbents. The two parties **"won't"** agree that the other side could run a good government. Neither will they agree to have a reduced and balanced budget. It is simply **"impossible"** for this to happen unless the existing Congress is renewed with all three classes replaced in the Senate and every House Representative that has served six years or more voted out. So if you are someone that's contradicting or just likes to think positive like me, and not use words like can't, won't or never, you can see why this is so important.

## Are We Dreamers Or Doers?

It's tough to replace even one person in Congress. If that person is part of the two-party system or backed financially by a partisan group, they will probably get re-elected. For decades we have been told by many "Sheeple" to vote for one of the two parties, or otherwise, your vote is wasted.

So, if you have been voting this way, you, my friend, are a dreamer. Let's be doers instead and get our one-third of the Senate and really refresh them with a couple of dozen newly elected freshmen.

The thought of replacing all of the Senators seems close to impossible. I say "close" because you have made it this far into the reading, which shows me that there is some hope. Sorry for all the boring repetition. I am ironically mimicking the approach of a politician: if something is said enough times and in different ways, it must be true.

The next step is to stop dreaming and to have a conversation with someone. Ask your friends, colleagues, and family if they think the only way to change Congress is to vote them out. Get ready to hear some strange responses. The reality is that no one has any idea how to make this happen. "Six Years and Out" has to be shared over and over again with our friends, relatives, and with our neighbors. We have to create what is called a groundswell of interest, and it has to be built on solid principles to work.

The familiar historical issue with elected officials is that they get privileges that they don't want to give up. They will never give up their perks unless they are voted out, die, or one of their peers threatens to expose some offense against the United States. One example points to the IRS incident in 2014 when the agency failed to fire Commissioner John Koskinen, who smugly proclaimed that he had nothing to apologize for when confronted with questions regarding the loss of emails on Lois Lerner's computer. The IRS made no move to react, even after Koskinen and Learner's inappropriate response to the ten Congressional hearings. This event was publicized on national television on June 20, 2014. If the same debacle had taken place in the private sector, Lerner and Koskinen would be fired on the spot. This episode is another example of how two parties who don't get along can't make a decision, and nobody has control of what's going on.

154

It's an insult to the intelligence of every American citizen when a public official blatantly, and publically lies about an issue that is transparent – in this case, withholding incriminating emails that were said to be lost due to a technical glitch. Today's Internet Service Providers [ISPs] are required by Federal Law to retain a copy of every record, even though this is directly in violation of Amendments 1,3,4,9, and 10, Let's not forget that the NSA also retains a copy of these records in the interest of national security.[53]

*"A people that values its privileges above its principles soon loses both."*

*--Dwight Eisenhower*

The term-limit concept you've been reading about has been in place since the writing of the Constitution. It was reinforced again through the adoption of the 17th Amendment in 1913, which declared that senators would be elected by the people and no longer appointed by state legislatures. If you have any interest in the true and fundamental meaning of the Constitution, and it would be well worth your time to read George Washington's farewell address. It is a tradition in the Senate to read it each year.

*"The new source of power is not money in the hands of a few, but information in the hands of many."*

*-- John Naisbitt*

It's our job to put this new source of power into the hands of many. This type of change can be brought about when like-minded people take it to the next step. We can start with the 34 states voting on the senate seats that expire this coming November in 2018.

New candidates for office should enter with a commitment to serve this country and its citizens for six years maximum. One of their promises should be to vacate office after their six-year term. I might suggest getting a copy of this book into the hands of the candidates that are up against the incumbents.

Once the "Six Years & Out" concept takes hold [I anticipate it will take twenty years or so], we might have a chance at writing an amendment to cement this principle. It truly would be the people that keep representatives to their six-year commitment until an amendment can be made into law. Ultimately, this Constitutional amendment would help to bring our republic back into its place by way of exercising our Democracy.

*"Be the change you want to see in the world."*

*-- Gandhi*

# Chapter Thirty

## Communication Was The Biggest Breakthrough In The History Of Humans

It was the desire for communication that enabled man to talk and then write in order to share knowledge. This innovation allowed humans to learn faster and survive longer. Communication allows us to build relationships with one another, and to structure our communities and societies with clear rules and standards for how we treat each other.

In our quest of changing Congress, it will take the power of today's rapid forms of communication to provide this knowledge to enough people. It doesn't need to take months or weeks to share the significance of term limits in the Constitution. We don't even have to take two to four days to mail this information or to broadcast it on the radio or television. With today's technology, sharing information can be done in the blink of an eye. People can share the thought, of *How To Replace Congress* by reaching out to thousands of people on Facebook or Twitter, all in a just a few seconds. Please take a moment right now and send the name of this book to one or two friends. Once enough voters have this information, they can make their own informed decision, and share the information with others. The good news is that although our choice of new candidates may still be limited, we have a wide array of candidates that we can choose not to vote for.

This book was written with the intention of being shared with as many fellow voters as possible so that we may eliminate any uncomfortable feelings about how we vote in senatorial elections. It's important to know that incumbents shouldn't be running for another term. Perhaps the important realization that senators must be chosen by the people, and must vacate their seats at the end of their term has not seeped into our political awareness since the major change was made in 1913.

157

As mentioned earlier, the 17<sup>th</sup> Amendment ensured that senators were to be elected to their posts by their constituents and not the state legislature. Despite this new law, we continue to allow legislators make all the decisions for us. Even if we want to argue the meaning of "shall vacate" the facts of replacing one-third of senators every two years makes too much sense not to do it. My father always advised me of his father's wise words, *"You should vote for the individual, not for the party."* Unfortunately, society has taught us that incumbents are candidates, when in fact, they should leave office.

Our legislative system for the people is a little more than broken, and so is the system that keeps legislators in office. It's our current legislators that leave it broken. What's worse is they have no idea of how to mend it. Our remodeled voting system was re-built to keep them in office, and until now, we had no idea of how to vote differently. Our two-party system does this intentionally so that each party has more power in government. Keeping them in office has the adverse effect of putting more power in the hands of a Congress that is disconnected from reality. Even agencies were initially slated to operate with a particular set of directives with a timeline of accomplishing them and with an end date for existence. They have all grown into virtually uncontrollable behemoths.

Despite a rather violent history of conflict mismanagement and secrecy, (there are too many examples to list, but they include the drug war in the United States, the War on Iraq, the countless school shootings, Oklahoma bombing, the unforgettable terrorist attacks of 9/11, and the assassinations of John Kennedy, Martin Luther King, Bobby Kennedy, and the shooting of Ronald Reagan), there are some people who argue that Congress is not to blame. Perhaps they are right. The finger of blame should be pointed at us, the voters. We are keeping these politicians in office, and it is up to use alone to make things right.

All of the above issues are controversial (many with conspiracy issues that can't be answered or won't be answered by the government) and it all goes back to our lack of leadership. Congress addresses domestic and international terrorism by creating more agencies, and more rules to stifle the freedom of its own citizens, rather than tackling the core of each problem in a responsible, honest, and transparent manner. While collecting research for this book, I spoke to many Americans who were willing to give up some of their freedom in return for the feeling of greater safety. How can we feel safe knowing that our military leaves billions of dollars worth of war equipment whey they retreat from war zones like Afghanistan?[54] How can we feel safer knowing that the US government has sold over 500,000 shoulder-launched surface-to-air missiles to various foreign governments and then almost entirely lost track of these deadly armaments as they fell into the hands of terrorist groups?[55]

This book is a plea to the people to use the intelligence and foresight of our forefathers. The authors of our Constitution knew that it would not make a difference to replace each individual in Congress one at a time. What they did know was that replacing one-third of senators at a time, we would have an efficient and collective outcome that would change the face of the majority in the Senate. Our forefathers thought of nearly everything, but even they could not predict such a thing as a bi-partisan party system. In fact, the Constitution didn't address a party system at all. I look at this as positive reinforcement that gives us room to make changes, even at this stage of the game. It's a good thing that the Constitution was not drafted by today's attorneys - for surely the ability to make a positive change would have been eliminated in the fine print.

# Chapter Thirty-One

## Going Viral

Mass media's ability to inform voters started out with flyers and newspapers. It was a slow and ineffective way to create a voters' movement. We have seen this method being used up to a few years ago in countries that had to rely on newspapers as a way of delivering information their citizens. As technology has advanced, the sound of news and propaganda traveled from home to home faster than ever via radio and television. Of course, these instruments were initially adopted only by the wealthy in "developed" countries, until many years later the wealth trickled down. Today, hundreds of millions of households around the world have a television set – and even more people have access to radio. Nonetheless, interested parties continued with their massive and mostly unwanted incumbent mailing campaigns (it's called *franking* in the U.S. costing Americans around 50 million dollars a year). In underdeveloped countries, paper propaganda along with censored radio and television advertisements are still the popular choice for politicians.

Today, Internet technology blankets the world allowing news and information to travel thousands of miles instantaneously. FYI, there are over 50 countries in the world with faster Internet than the United States. This type of media power is what has helped several countries and their people understand that new leadership can take the place of tyranny.

But the Internet alone did not accomplish all this. The key factor was the will of the people who had a desire to erase corruption from their politics. They took their passion to the Internet, and the desire for responsible government and liberty went viral, allowing the message to be heard around the world. It will take no less desire to abolish corruption within the United States.

160

To make this happen, we need this powerful message to go viral in America.

For those that are unaware of what "going viral" refers to, it is the phenomenon where information is shared with millions of people in a very short period. So it is up to the voters to spread the word to other voters and non-voters, and for each of us to make our own decision on whether political corruption exists or not. If we concede that corruption exists, the process can be changed. The bleak alternative is to continue ignoring the problem, which appears to be leading to a deterioration of America's political system. I believe most Americans love this country, and this is a way to save it.

At least for today, the Internet in America is still an open domain with the freedom to share thoughts and challenge ideas. Even in the US, we are beginning to see potential provocations to our freedom of the Internet due to the questionable massive data retention laws. Luckily, our digital freedom has not been as restricted as in countries like Russia, North Korea, and China.

## Making it Reassuring

This book is not about changing our Constitution – it's a suggestion that we should start living by its rules. The Constitution is fluid that's clear; it was also created as the law of how the government was to operate. What's also clear is that it was built to protect and govern the people through the decisions of "elected" officials chosen by the people. Having chosen our legislators, we the people have the responsibility to check their records and balance their indiscretions with corrections. We currently entrust the Supreme Court to make the final decisions on what is constitutiona even though this court of justices is appointed, not elected, by the two parties.

We need to check our party affiliation and ask ourselves a tough question, **is it time that we start voting for what's good for America?** Or, should we let legislation continue to find ways to create federal laws that take those rights away?

There is a growing problem of our personal privacy being at an even greater risk in the United States. As this is being written, federal law monitors and stores our websites and our emails. Our rights of privacy are taken away by heavy-handed national security. For those people that don't use the Internet, they would be surprised - or should I say shocked - what the Internet knows about them. The Internet has a file on all of us, whether we want it to or not.

Stalking was mentioned earlier in the book. I believe a closer look needs to taken from the seemingly harmless GPS on our phone systems (even the flip phones have this unwanted feature). The definition: • *"harass or persecute (someone) with unwanted and obsessive attention.* We always have to remember there is a human factor involved with knowing where we are at any given moment and any routine that we as individuals have. The good: let's us know how to find restaurants, gas stations, hotels and more. These are helpful and desired reasons to have such a device.

The bad: how many different sinister ways this same technology could bring harm against us or our loved ones. They always know when you are not home, on vacation, away from your car and even worse away from your family. If you have any children or elderly parents with these type of devices someone also knows when they are most vulnerable. From a terrorist standpoint they would know which group of people have gathered, what time, day and how often. We need to understand that this information is being shared but it can also be hacked. You may not be doing anything wrong and don't care. This could be called clueless and maybe off-guard and unprepared.

162

# Chapter Thirty-Two

## Technology Is On Our Side

The Internet can help us if we optimize its power. Facebook, Twitter, Blogs, LinkedIn and e-mail can help spread this message. We can change almost anything thousands of times faster. Nonetheless, the National Security Agency (NSA) has and could act in ways that could impact how and what we communicate. Currently, the NSA is operating with some caution due to Edward Snowden's release of NSA secrets to the world, such as their recording all of our emails, web searches, phone conversations, and even our home-recorded videos. It seems that our big government is acting a little more like N. Korea every day, and intentionally suppressing what their citizens can do.

Leaving computers open to backdoor intrusions is no small concern. Twenty-five percent of Canadian businesses with operations in the United States are moving data outside of the U.S. as a result of privacy scandals. Verizon is a company that adds significantly to the problem. Verizon has granted the government so much access to customer records that they don't even know what the NSA is accessing on a daily basis, nor is anyone notified that their private information was obtained.[56]

## Did The Telecommunications Industry Pull Off An Extremely Cunning And Monumentally Expensive Con On America?

One entity has been allowed to monopolize the majority of the telephone system (now including mobile networks) in order to build our massive communication system.

It took the United States over 100 years to get 300 million people connected to a network that was regulated as a monopoly. All the poles, lines, phones, and services needed to be connected to provide phone service across state borders, mountain ranges, and deserts. All of this has been paid for a few times over by consumers like you and i. So who really owns this equipment? In 1982, one of the largest companies in American history, AT&T, was broken up because it essentially had complete control over all communication in the United States.

They were too big to handle as a regulated monopoly. Then, in less than two decades cellular innovation brought phone service to billions of people worldwide. Now if legislation allowed it, wireless technology would make cellular services outdated at a fraction of the cost. [See the 2009 Broadband America Act passed by Congress that has never been implemented]. Giving America much more inexpensive forms of communication should be at the top of government's agenda. Cellular devices are the most used form of communication today. Wi-Fi should be everywhere in the Untied States and can be provided at a very low cost.

## The Con

Modern day monopolization of communication has quickly changed. Just a handful of companies provide landline and cellular phone service, as well as Internet, TV, and GPS. Verizon, Comcast and other large telecoms took control and bundled these services, single-handedly reaching well over one hundred million people in the U.S. Now they provide virtually uncontrolled cost for cellular, the Internet, and television service [or collusive services] larger than AT&T. It took billions of dollars' worth of lobbying to pull this con on the American people in order to have exclusive control within the cellular industry.

The giant telecoms are now making billions on these non-regulated services while charging civilians exorbitant prices. We could provide broadband to all Americans at a tenth of the cost of your current plan, even with a smartphone. An example of a more cost effective plan is Republicwireless.com. They provide unlimited talk, text and data on the latest state of the art smartphone for less than $15 per month, including taxes and fees. I recently spoke with a customer service rep from Amazon that was from Costa Rica. They only pay $20 a month for a smartphone with all of the features. Wake up America, please, this is a Con!

Only a new Congress could revise these unregulated telecom monopolies that are guaranteed a profit by public service commissions (PSC). If America went wireless, then Internet, TV, GPS, radio, cellular phones and other services could be provided to you nearly free in a very similar way that television was provided for over fifty years.

FYI, all these technologies are radio waves and all of them travel at a speed of light. Just wanted to put that thought in your head as you are wondering which one is faster than the other. That smartphone I talked about from Republic Wireless is a Wi-Fi phone; a cell phone, a computer, a GPS, a TV, a radio and all with unlimited access. Now you see why we should "broadband" America. We all know that nothing is free; but how many times do we have to pay for the same satellites and base stations?

The High Definition television was forced on us. This change happened when lobbyist gave us no choice by having legislation passed to eliminate existing television frequencies. We either bought a new TV or placed set-top converter on our old one. Of course, the third choice is to forgo the TV entirely. Is this starting to sound like a huge con game? Remember, this game started with cable TV, which dazzled us with promises of doing away with commercials. Now we have Smart TV's which force us to have the Internet.

These days, almost no one under the age of forty-five or over the age of eighty realizes that you can get HD TV with an antenna. As a result, just a small demographic of people remains that would be open to new possibilities. A telecom's worst nightmare is if their average customer realized that GPS and wireless Internet are available to the public for free. Throw in the low-cost smartphone and we can finally do away with those $200-a-month phone, Internet, and cable bills. You can begin to see why telecoms spend tens of millions of dollars to keep legislators in office. We really don't need them, if America goes wireless. We are beginning to see a shift already with low-cost monthly subscriptions to web-based TV series and movies providers, and even channels like ESPN and HBO giving on-the-go access or a fee. Even so, we should still remember the huge amount of content that used to be provided for free by channels like NBC, ABC, FOX, and other public stations.

In the face of such an unmistakable monopoly, where is the head of the Federal Communication Commission (FCC-aka bureaucrat, defined as an administrator concerned with the procedural correctness of the people's needs) and Congress (aka legislators, defined as lawmakers and managers of bureaucrats)? Perhaps the real question is, how much are they being paid or "donated" that allows these massive, out-of-control telecommunications PAC's to take advantage of people so blatantly? How were enough people able to agree to this massive and wide range of deception brought on to America?

Using Florida as an example, Verizon was deregulated in the cellular, Internet, television, and GPS services offered to consumers. Florida's legislation voted to allow this in 2011, with zero benefits to the citizens of Florida. Now, the state's residents face an uncontrollably higher monthly cost for these services. Comcast is another major player, said to have the seventh largest lobbying budget of any single company or organization in the United States (rumor is that they spent $18 million lobbying in 2013).

Repealing these deregulatory laws will be impossible unless the people of Florida vote out their entire state legislation. The legislators who voted for Verizon to monopolize communications in the state will not admit any fault. According to ABC News, Verizon Communications has reached a decision to shed its traditional telephone line business in 14 states in a deal worth $8.6 billion.[57] Customers who had Verizon FiOS internet, Cable TV, or phone services with Verizon in states like Texas, California, and Florida are automatically switched to a company called Frontier Communications. What kind of political money is at play to get a bill of this magnitude passed through Congress? There is no doubt that a decision to take away the fundamental right of choice from Americans set off a chain reaction echoing across the country's service providers.

If you were wondering, lobbying by Verizon worked extremely well in FL, as both Democrats and Republicans in Florida all voted for this extremely costly piece of legislation[56]. In a conversation with the Florida Public Service Commission, we checked how Florida's legislators voted - as this information is available to the public. What we've concluded is that Verizon has a lot of money. I always question if we really learn from history. Didn't we learn anything from the debacles with AT&T or Microsoft?

The lesson to be gleaned from our history is such;, when a company has a locked-in customer base (a monopoly) they can raise their price a little each month whenever they want. They can also keep out competition by lobbying federal legislation (in this case the FCC). Likewise, a federal or state agency cannot exist without the industry they "regulate." So each agency and corresponding industries have unusual closed-door relationships. Together they make sure that each party gets what the other needs. If you'd like to test this theory, pick any federal agency and find the industry that it oversees.

What you will find is that the industry wants to keep competition out, and the agency wants to become larger and "more important." Do we need either one of these options? Which federal or state body will determine who will lead this agency? We stumble upon yet another reason why Congress should not be bought and influenced by the PACs who are controlled by the very agencies they aim to influence. We want representatives that oversee the budget and operations of every agency in agreement with the "checks and balances" system created to keep every chamber of our government under control.

# Chapter Thirty-Three

## Solving Problems by Consensus

The consensus is very different than the archaic verbal "yea" and "nay" voting system currently used by Congress when voting on a bill. Some bills require a two-thirds vote, but with this old-world and outdated "yea" and "nay" system, it's more of a mob-rule way of voting. The first thing that congressmen do when they come together on the floor is they verbally oppose the other party. Why verbally? Because the party that controls either house gets the most "yea's" and that's how a vote is made. Individual congressmen may vote "nay" when their party didn't bring the action or bill to the floor. Conversely, if their party wrote the action or bill, it would get a "yea" or yes vote. It's easy to see why there is power number on the senate floor!

Consensus, on the other hand, is a way for a group of people to come to an agreement when approving an idea. It is about saying or agreeing that we can collectively live with the accepted solution until something better comes along. With the help of consensus, an agreement can be made no matter which party brings it to the floor. In this manner, Congress could be working together rather than taking sides. "Problem Solving by Consensus," is a form of decision-making based on common sense, reasoning, and acting with integrity.

I know this is clearly a stretch when they currently have to listen to the House or Senate leaders dictating how everyone should vote. Our senators and representatives should be voting for what their state constituents want and not what their party or PACs, desire.

By using consensus, our legislators could be contributing and building on new ideas and opinions that allow problems to be solved. Instead of having a winner and a loser in each debate, we can create win/win situations by consenting to a better solution  - all for the good of the

American people. Yes, it is in the Constitution, but that was also before they had electricity and could drive to work. So what we've been getting instead is a two-party system that keeps adding language to bills and is unwilling to compromise.

## A Stuck Congress Is A Lame-Duck Congress

Sylvester Stallone weighs in on politics, saying, "*I don't think you can be totally one-sided forever. Then you close your mind to all sorts of possibilities. It's just, 'Who comes along better at that time of what the planet is going through?' Right now, it's pretty confusing on every side.*" [58] If we can all vote on those measures, we would not have the bi-partisan issues that plague our government today.

The so-called "Lame Duck Congress" is the result of our infamous opposing-party-system that is in its very nature programmed to disagree. That system works well only if one's plan of action is to delay legislation or not get anything done. These two opposing parties label each other with belittling names like "conservative" or "liberal," "right wing" and "left wing." If we continue to vote using a two-party system, it reduces the very foundation of having a voice of having 100 senators and 435 representatives down to two? Yes, the two-party system has filtered the 535 members of Congress down to basically two parties, and by doing so, they have taken away our fair representation in government.

A small group of people who control an entire country is defined as an oligarchy.  What's regretful is that people have a hard time differentiating between the two different political parties because of their centralist platforms that are designed to appeal to the largest possible constituency.

170

Here is what we know with certainty: the political system won't change itself, and it won't make itself smaller. History continues to show us that it truly doesn't matter which party claims that they will change the government or reduce its size - neither ever takes place. When will we learn this from history?

So how do we get new people into Congress that use common sense, reasoning, and also have integrity? First don't look to career politicians. As soon as you start to hear about his or her political experience, look for someone else to vote for. If you pay close attention to the comments made during elections, you will be amazed at their incoherence. During the current presidential race in 2016, we hear such banter, as **"that person doesn't have presidential experience."** What are the commentators trying to imply with this phrase? **Must the candidate have been a president for some other country first before daring to run for the same office in America?** Really, what a comment!

I have been told so many times, "Well, when you articulate it that way, what we need to do is just not to vote for these individuals anymore**." Poof, common sense just kicked in.** The only way for us to get career politicians out of office is by not re-electing them. We can do this gradually by voting out one-third of senators every two years. We must avoid re-electing any incumbent after their six-year term is up! This opportunity comes along only once every six years for each of our state senators. As a reminder, an entire class of senators should be replaced every two years.

We can simultaneously check the length of time any House Representative has been in office. If their service spans six years or longer, they need a break from *not* serving us so hard. Kind of a sad oxymoron isn't it?

# Chapter Thirty-Four

## Being Open-Minded

To consider that there is a better way to doing anything is a start. The next step is to make a small commitment to be part of the change. There is that old cliché, "either you are part of the problem, or you are part of the solution".

I have found people to be extremely interested and non-confrontational when bringing up the possibility of being able to change Congress. The challenge will be to determine how many people give talking about politics a chance? People are very dissatisfied with Congress and are ready to make a change Let's start by replacing the 16 senators that have been in office for 18 years or longer. If we can also replace 1/3 of the representatives in the House who have served more than 18 years, including the majority leaders, and we would have the accomplishment to celebrate.

Asking the parties to provide candidates instead of incumbents is not going to be well received. We must ask them by showing our discontent, and we can do that by not voting for incumbents. We would also be sending a clear message to career politicians by not voting them back into office and replacing them with fresh blood. This message is not about selling books; it's about helping the world, by showing that America is still a country to be admired by millions of people and continues to be a role model to follow for other nations. Let's be open to the idea that other countries' voters will be inspired by our accomplishment and follow our lead.

Talking about politics is challenging at best. But we have an opportunity to remove some of the corruption that seems so inherent in politics, and to bring fresh ideas to the table.

172

Let me expound. Fresh ideas are not those of the Rick Perry, Hillary Clinton, Chris Christie, Russ Feingold or Scott Walker, to name a few. These are names that people bring up when talking politics in a negative way. There will be an even longer list of career politicians who try to claim that they are new and different – that list will be created by readers like you once word gets out about "Six Years and Out." Or, you can just look up the list of politicians convicted of crimes in Wikipedia. The point is that none of the abovementioned incumbents have "any" criminal record, just that the longer in office, the more tainted one becomes.

# Chapter Thirty-Five

## Why Do We Need To Vote This New Way?

At the time of writing, there are at least 27 states that will not allow you to vote for the candidate of your choice regardless of their party affiliation, but rather force you to vote along party lines. You can be a registered voter, and show up on Election Day during the primaries and not be allowed to vote. Does that seem strange to you? These states are contributing to the voting problem by allowing legislators create rules that keep them in office. As a result, when elections come around our trusty political parties only offer us a list of incumbents from their side and not a viable list of contenders for office. Clearly, this is a limit on our freedom of choice. The only entities that benefit in this case are the parties themselves, the incumbent, and unfortunately the super PACs. The losers, in this instance, are you, and I. It sounds wrong because it is wrong.

## Our Right To Vote Has Been Taken Away

Our right to vote has been taken away by either State or Federal Laws - and these laws are unjust. Many similar laws are a minimum of thirty years old. If not for the antiquity and impracticality of our House of Representatives and the Senate, the unjust laws would have already been overturned.

This violation of eliminating our freedom of choice also supports the need for replacing one-third of Congress every two years. If we don't take this crucial step, those laws remain to be an example of how it will be impossible to overturn any legislature without new lawmakers in office. If you don't do this for you, do it for your children, and their children.

Needless to say, each legislator that we are going to vote for was already chosen exclusively by our two-party system. You might see a politician from another party trying to replace the politician from the opposite party, but they are still politicians. Most of us believe parties would be of more value if they brought us competition instead of incumbents. At this time, any single person who would like to run for office is unable to do so, so long as their party already has an incumbent that is going after the same position. In order to be able to run for office, one would have to switch parties entirely, or not run at all. How, one might ask, does switching sides make your party stronger and help your platform? There is no sense or reason here. Recognizing this dilemma is the first step. The solution s to move forward by not voting for incumbents.

## Is Voting More Difficult Than Being an Illegal Immigrant?

Being able to vote in America is becoming more and more difficult. Some of this difficulty comes as a form of protection against voter fraud. Ironically, it is easier for an illegal immigrant to get a social security number, driver's license, fake birth certificate, send their children to our schools, and use social welfare and health care in our country than it is for a legal citizen to vote non-partisan.

Our government not only took the Pledge of Allegiance out of schools but now Congress has also forsaken their pledge of loyalty to American citizens. With Congress' performance at an all time low for the last twenty years or more, we now know how to elect a governing body that can do better than its predecessors. This next comment shouldn't even come as a surprise. PAC money contributors don't care which party is in office! A bold, but true statement - yet have you ever seen a reduction in the size of government, fewer wars, less corruption, more whistle blowing on their peers, or fewer bureaucrats?

Of course not, but our legislators' game was up a long time ago. Now it's the voters' turn to act, by starting the replacement process of our failed Congress. Our party system as failed us, and it's time to get back to our roots.

We might liken this political purging to cleaning up the gangs in the inner cities or helping to extinguish fires using out of state firefighters or volunteers. Lack of new leadership has become a societal issue that has been allowed to run out of control. If you vote, please look at the whole picture, not just at how someone might address a particular issue. If a political candidate is an incumbent, consider their political duties completed in full. If they want another chance, we're suggesting that they wait ten years before they can put their name on a campaign list.

Hillary is an example of how the party system doesn't work. She barely has any Democratic competition. Do they really think it's because no other Democrat wants to be President? Mr. Trump could have gone to either party, but instead, he used his intelligence to take on the Republican Party first. It's a good decision for several reasons. One of the most obvious reasons is the following logic. If you look at history, it tells us that after two consecutive terms as President, the probability that the opposing party will win the next election is very high. He would have beat Hillary by the second debate, so he knew beating the Republican Party first would put him in the oval office. Trump is not a politician; he's a Patriot.

So who has a better chance at turning around our political slump than someone that politicians hate and someone that is willing to say what a politician won't? Throughout Trump's campaign, the Republican Party has challenged his candidacy. Trump could have elected to run as an independent, but perhaps he anticipates that people will be more receptive to him if he plays on the side of the party. Hillary, on the other hand, has the strength of female and minority supporters, as well as the Clinton name to back her up.

176

This dichotomy can be attributed to the broken two-party system. Talking Presidential elections may be good for conversation, but we don't actually vote for the president, so let's stick to putting out fires and making the best of our situation.

In this scenario, we are the "firefighters" or patriots and Congress is the fire or loyalist. We need to combine resources, use our vote, and start the process of replacing career politicians. The first fire is the first third of Congress. Putting out this fire should be a relatively easy task because it does not even require us to leave our community. After one successful year of not voting for incumbents, the parties will quickly adjust their sights on real candidates for the next election. They need to know that Americans are serious about this agenda. We can prove this by beginning to vote them out every even-numbered year.

# Chapter Thirty-Six

## So How Can We Start Making a Change?

Spread the word. We must emphasize that we need to be voting out our overdue incumbents every even-numbered year. Those who have served six years in a political role have exhausted their right to continue to play a part in politics. They've served their role in society, and now they must step aside. As you go about your day and have conversations with different people, keep the "Six Years and Out" message in mind. Share the critical passage in Article I, Section 3 with your family, friends, and neighbors, and tell them that it's time to vote for fresh minds. Hopefully, these fresh minds will not bring political corruption with them. I recommend that we vote not for politicians or American Royalty, but rather for those unique civilians who want to be Public Servants.

Extend your reach outside your immediate circle of family and friends. Contacting your high school or university graduating class is easier than ever with well-connected school networks. Remember, you don't have to be a politician to serve this country. You need to have integrity, a will to move America forward in a timely manner, and the foresight to work with people who may not have the same view and opinions come from the same neighborhood or state, or even from the same party. Reaching out to our friends, colleagues, and family via social media networks comes as second nature for many of us. I would strongly encourage you to post your thoughts on the upcoming elections, not with the intent of stirring up another bi-partisan debate, but rather to introduce a new idea and fresh perspective.

Many of your friends and followers will probably be shocked to discover that for the last hundred years we were able to vote for new officials on each even-numbered year.

178

Remind them that there are 33 Class I, 33 Class II or 34 Class III Senators who can be voted out. These career politicians are attempting to get re-elected when they should be vacating office. "Six Years and Out" makes it easy to remember when we go to vote. A new Congress can only truly be "new" if one-third of the Senate is replaced each voting year.

Remind your network that if we begin voting this way in November 2016, we could substitute 34 Class III Senators. In two years in 2018, 33 Class I senators, and 33 Class II Senators in 2020. Following this pattern would allow us to replace all 100 U.S. Senators every six years. Two years later, we start the process over. It's as simple as voting.

## What's Insanity?

Let your friends and family know that they do have a choice. They could choose to do nothing – like 60% of all eligible voters during midterm elections. Or, they can continue voting for the incumbent - like 40% of our constituents currently vote in midterm elections. Remind your network that doing nothing will bring the same results. But doing the same thing over and over again would truly be irrational. Albert Einstein once said,

> *"Doing the same thing over and over again and expecting different results is the mark of insanity."* -- Albert Einstein

If the 40% of the midterm voters are unhappy with how ineffective Congress is then, we have some real hope for change. When they hear about "Six Years and Out," at least 50% of these unhappy voters will use the methods described in this book and, begin electing a new Congress.

If you still have doubt that being in office too long breeds corruption and absolute power, I urge you to look to the leaders of other countries, and all the unrest and terror there is throughout the world as a result.

At some point, you might have heard or said the phrase, "The United States of America has the best democracy, in the world." Perhaps this statement has some truth to it. So much so, that other countries have used our Constitution as a foundation to form their government. The other day, I had an eye-opening chat with a customer service individual from South Africa. He confessed to me that in his country, they had a democracy, and yet the silent majority always elects their leadership. This conversation illustrates an excellent example of a political system that we do not want. It could be said that their leaders are elected by the Parliament of South Africa rather than by the people. I found it interesting in its own way that the United States Electoral College seems like the silent majority. Ever wonder if they already have chosen who will be the next President in 2016?

# Summary

Life is full of tough choices. *How To Replace Congress* shouldn't be one of them. Nonetheless, lack of time, research, or even access to information has made the voting decision tough for many people. It is also tough to overcome the fact that the Greatest Country in the world could possibly use improvements. There isn't a country in the world that doesn't have corruption; our Congress is not an exception.

*How To Replace Congress* is bringing together years of research in order to make it easier for you to vote while intelligently overcoming objections to your choice of candidate. By design, this book will also make it easier for you to share the message with others, and choose "Six Years and Cut."

The next several pages list the names of politicians that have been in office for six years or longer. Some have been in office since Presidents Johnson, Nixon, Ford, Carter, Reagan, HW Bush, Clinton, GW Bush and Obama... you get the idea - a long time. They don't have a good track record of policing themselves or the Presidents. They have not done a good job as mentors for other legislators, and they don't deserve to continue serving in any political office. Existing legislators need to take sufficient amount of time to prove that they can live productively in the societal system that they have created.

If we want better choices for candidates, we need to make room for them in Congress. For change in legislation, there must be a charge in legislators. Let's pave the way to replace one-third of Congressional seats in the House and Senate every two years with non-politicians. Let's look at the roots of our nation and to the principles of the Constitution in order to address the core problems occurring in our country today.

It is our only hope to not only get our rights back but also to bring jobs back to America, have a smaller government, reduce taxes, protect our borders, clean up our own streets, to rebuild our infrastructures throughout the country and to pay back our national debt. To see the American dream become a reality once again, use your vote wisely– use *How To Replace Congress.*

# Appendix A

## Check Your State to See Who Not To Vote For

The following is a compilation of many hours of research for a list of Class III Senators listed by State in alphabetical order. There are cnly 34 States [numbered 1 -34 and highlighted in bold]. These are the only 34 States that vote for a Senator in 2016. All 50 Sates listed alphabetical a list of their House of Representative and the district they represent. That district number is next to each state.

All have been in office from 6 to 40 years. Yes, there are 334 names on this list. **We are long overdue for replacing old, dusty politicians, for brand-new public servants.** This books attempt is to show you how our continued way of voting for incumbents has been the reason our government is in such a mess. I know from talking to hundreds of people that they only think about how their vote for their favorite incumbent won't do any harm. Take a closer look at how every-bodies one vote has had such a dramatic impact on doing the same thing and expecting different results.

Since you may be from one of the sixteen states that only get's one vote in 2016 please try and get this message to someone in one of thirty-four states that have Class III Senators.

## The Following 34 States Have Class III Senators:

1.Alabama, 2.Alaska, 3.Arizona, 4.Arkansas, 5.California, 6.Colorado, 7.Connecticut, 8.Florida, 9.Georgia, 10.Hawaii, 11.Idaho, 12.Illinois, 13.Indiana, 14.Iowa, 15.Kansas, 16.Kentucky, 17.Louisiana, 18.Maryland, 19.Missouri, 20.Nevada, 21.New Hampshire, 22.New York, 23.North

Carolina, 24.North Dakota, 25.Ohio, 26.Oklahoma, 27.Oregon, 28.Pennsylvania, 29.South Carolina, 30.South Dakota, 31.Utah, 32.Vermont, 33.Washington, 34.Wisconsin.

You may also want to share this with anyone you might know in any of the following areas because many of these people have been in office for Twenty years or more!

35.District of Columbia, 36.American Samoa, 37.Guam, 38.Northern Mariana Islands, 39.Puerto Rico, 40.The Virgin Islands.

The next four pages is a list of people that have or appeared to have chosen politics as a career. They have all served six years or longer as of the November 2016 elections. It was created to be as accurate as possible; the attempt was to cite career politicians and other legislators that have served six years or longer. If you are in agreement that six years and out will help to limit corruption, then not voting for the following people should also make sense. Individuals that genuinely chose to be public servants instead of politicians would also agree with this ideology, as they are representing the people's freedom of choice.

## Corruption

One note regarding the use of the word "corruption" in the book; the author does not use it to imply that any of the people listed are dishonest. Rather the idea is that our existing political system changes the behavior, the action or response of how people will or will not make decisions while in office and that most of them receive outside PAC money to get re-elected.

The information on these pages is a compilation sourced from the following sites:

www.house.gov/,http://www.senate.gov/index.htm

wikipedia.org/wiki/List_of_current_members_of_the_United_States_House_of_Representatives_by_age

| # | | District | Name | # | | District | Name |
|---|---|---|---|---|---|---|---|
| 1 | 1 | **Alabama** | **Richard Shelby** | 48 | | California 48 | Dana Rohrabacher |
| 2 | | Alabama 2 | Martha Roby | 49 | | California 49 | Darrell Issa |
| 3 | | Alabama 3 | Mike D. Rogers | 50 | | California 50 | Duncan D. Hunter |
| 4 | | Alabama 4 | Robert Aderholt | 51 | | California 53 | Susan A. Davis |
| 5 | | Alabama 5 | Mo Brooks | 52 | 6 | **Colorado** | **Michael Bennet** |
| 6 | | Alabama 7 | Terri Sewell | 53 | | Colorado 1 | Diana DeGette |
| 7 | 2 | **Alaska** | **Lisa Murkowski** | 54 | | Colorado 2 | Jared Polis |
| 8 | | Alaska | Don Young | 55 | | Colorado 3 | Scott Tipton |
| 9 | 3 | **Arizona** | **John McCain** | 56 | | Colorado 5 | Doug Lamborn |
| 10 | | Arizona 3 | Raul Grijalva | 57 | | Colorado 6 | Mike Coffman |
| 11 | | Arizona 4 | Paul Gosar | 58 | | Colorado 7 | Ed Perlmutter |
| 12 | | Arizona 6 | David Schweikert | 59 | 7 | **Connecticut** | **Richard Blumenthal** |
| 13 | | Arizona 8 | Trent Franks | 60 | | Connecticut 1 | John B. Larson |
| 14 | 4 | **Arkansas** | **John Boozman** | 61 | | Connecticut 2 | Joe Courtney |
| 15 | | Arkansas 1 | Rick Crawford | 62 | | Connecticut 3 | Rosa DeLauro |
| 16 | | Arkansas 3 | Steve Womack | 63 | | Connecticut 4 | Jim Himes |
| 17 | 5 | **California** | **Barbara Boxer** | 64 | | Delaware | John Carney |
| 18 | | California 3 | John Garamendi | 65 | 8 | **Florida** | **Marco Rubio** |
| 19 | | California 4 | Tom McClintock | 66 | | Florida 1 | Mike Coffman |
| 20 | | California 5 | Mike Thompson | 67 | | Florida 4 | Ander Crenshaw |
| 21 | | California 6 | Doris Matsui | 68 | | Florida 5 | Corrine Brown |
| 22 | | California 9 | Jerry McNerney | 69 | | Florida 7 | John Mica |
| 23 | | California 10 | Jeff Denham | 70 | | Florida 8 | Bill Posey |
| 24 | | California 12 | Nancy Pelosi | 71 | | Florida 10 | Daniel Webster |
| 25 | | California 13 | Barbara Lee | 72 | | Florida 12 | Ed Perlmutter |
| 26 | | California 14 | Jackie Speier | 73 | | Florida 14 | John B. Larson |
| 27 | | California 16 | Jim Costa | 74 | | Florida 16 | Joe Courtney |
| 28 | | California 17 | Mike Honda | 75 | | Florida 17 | Tom J. Rooney |
| 29 | | California 18 | Anna Eshoo | 76 | | Florida 20 | Alcee Hastings |
| 30 | | California 19 | Zoe Lofgren | 77 | | Florida 21 | Ted Deutch |
| 31 | | California 20 | Sam Farr | 78 | | Florida 23 | Debbie Wasserman Schultz |
| 32 | | California 22 | Devin Nunes | 79 | | Florida 24 | Frederica Wilson |
| 33 | | California 23 | Kevin McCarthy | 80 | | Florida 25 | Mario Diaz-Balart |
| 34 | | California 24 | Lois Capps | 81 | | Florida 27 | Ileana Ros-Lehtinen |
| 35 | | California 27 | Judy chu | 82 | 9 | **Georgia** | **Johnny Isakson** |
| 36 | | California 28 | Adam Schiff | 83 | | Georgia 2 | Sanford Bishop |
| 37 | | California 30 | Brad Sherman | 84 | | Georgia 3 | Lynn Westmoreland |
| 38 | | California 32 | Grace Napolitano | 85 | | Georgia 4 | Hank Johnson |
| 39 | | California 34 | Xavier Becerra | 86 | | Georgia 5 | John R. Lewis |
| 40 | | California 37 | Karen Bass | 87 | | Georgia 6 | Tom Price |
| 41 | | California 38 | Linda Sanchez | 88 | | Georgia 7 | Rob Woodall |
| 42 | | California 39 | Ed Royce | 89 | | Georgia 8 | Austin Scott |
| 43 | | California 40 | Lucille Roybal-Allard | 90 | | Georgia 13 | David Scott |
| 44 | | California 42 | Ken Calvert | 91 | | Georgia 14 | Tom Graves |
| 45 | | California 43 | Maxine Waters | 92 | 10 | **Hawaii** | **Brian Schatz** |
| 46 | | California 44 | Janice Hahn | 93 | 11 | **Idaho** | **Mike Crapo** |
| 47 | | California 46 | Loretta Sanchez | 94 | | Idaho 1 | Raul Labrador |
| | | | | 95 | | Idaho 2 | Mike Simpson |

186

| | | | |
|---|---|---|---|
| 96 | 12 | Illinois | **Mark Kirk** |
| 97 | | Illinois 1 | Bobby Rush |
| 98 | | Illinois 3 | Dan Lipinski |
| 99 | | Illinois 4 | Luis Gutiérrez |
| 100 | | Illinois 5 | Michael Quigley |
| 101 | | Illinois 6 | Peter Roskam |
| 102 | | Illinois 7 | Danny K. Davis |
| 103 | | Illinois 9 | Jan Schakowsky |
| 104 | | Illinois 14 | Randy Hultgren |
| 105 | | Illinois 15 | John Shimkus |
| 106 | | Illinois 16 | Adam Kinzinger |
| 107 | 13 | **Indiana** | **Dan Coats** |
| 108 | | Indiana 1 | Pete Visclosky |
| 109 | | Indiana 3 | Marlin Stutzman |
| 110 | | Indiana 4 | Todd Rokita |
| 111 | | Indiana 7 | André Carson |
| 112 | | Indiana 8 | Larry Bucshon |
| 113 | | Indiana 9 | Todd Young |
| 114 | 14 | **Iowa** | **Chuck Grassley** |
| 115 | | Iowa 2 | David Loebsack |
| 116 | | Iowa 4 | Steve King |
| 117 | 15 | **Kansas** | **Jerry Moran** |
| 118 | | Kansas 1 | Time Huelskamp |
| 119 | | Kansas 2 | Lynn Jenkins |
| 120 | | Kansas 3 | Kevin Yoder |
| 121 | | Kansas 4 | Mike Pompeo |
| 122 | 16 | **Kentucky** | **Paul Rand** |
| 123 | | Kentucky 1 | Ed Whitfield |
| 124 | | Kentucky 2 | Brett Guthrie |
| 125 | | Kentucky 3 | John Yarmuth |
| 126 | | Kentucky 5 | Hal Rogers |
| 127 | 17 | **Louisiana** | **David Vitter** |
| 128 | | Louisiana 1 | Steve Scalise |
| 129 | | Louisiana 2 | Cedric Richmond |
| 130 | | Louisiana 3 | Charles Boustany |
| 131 | | Louisiana 4 | John C. Fleming |
| 132 | | Maine 1 | Chellie Pingree |
| 133 | 18 | **Maryland** | **Barbara Mikulski** |
| 134 | | Maryland 1 | Andrew P. Harris |
| 135 | | Maryland 2 | Dutch Ruppersberger |
| 136 | | Maryland 3 | John Sarbanes |
| 137 | | Maryland 4 | Donna Edwards |
| 138 | | Maryland 5 | Steny Hoyer |
| 139 | | Maryland 7 | Elijah Cummings |
| 140 | | Maryland 8 | Chris Van Hollen |
| 141 | | Massachusetts 1 | Richard Neal |
| 142 | | Massachusetts 2 | Jim McGovern |
| 143 | | Massachusetts 3 | Nikki Tsongas |
| 144 | | Massachusetts 8 | Stephen F. Lynch |
| 145 | | Massachusetts 9 | William R. Keating |
| 146 | | Michigan 1 | Dan Benishek |
| 147 | | Michigan 2 | Bill Huizerga |
| 148 | | Michigan | Justin Amash |
| 149 | | Michigan 6 | Fred Upton |
| 150 | | Michigan 7 | Tim Walberg |
| 151 | | Michigan 8 | Mike J. Rogers |
| 152 | | Michigan 9 | Sander M. Levin |
| 153 | | Michigan 10 | Candice Miller |
| 154 | | Michigan 13 | John Conyers |
| 155 | | Minnesota | Al Franken |
| 156 | | Minnesota 1 | Tim Walz |
| 157 | | Minnesota 2 | John Kline |
| 158 | | Minnesota 3 | Erik Paulsen |
| 159 | | Minnesota 4 | Betty McCollum |
| 160 | | Minnesota 5 | Keith Ellison |
| 161 | | Minnesota 7 | Collin Peterson |
| 162 | | Mississippi 2 | Bennie Thompson |
| 163 | | Mississippi 3 | Gregg Harper |
| 164 | | Mississippi 4 | Steven Palazzo |
| 165 | 19 | **Missouri** | **Roy Blunt** |
| 166 | | Missouri 1 | William L. Clay, Jr. |
| 167 | | Missouri 3 | Blaine Luetkemeyer |
| 168 | | Missouri 4 | Vicky Hartzer |
| 169 | | Missouri 5 | Emanuel Cleaver |
| 170 | | Missouri 6 | Sam Graves |
| 171 | | Missouri 8 | Jason T. Smith |
| 172 | | Nebraska | Mike Johanns |
| 173 | | Nebraska 1 | Jeff Fortenberry |
| 174 | | Nebraska 3 | Adrian M. Smith |
| 175 | 20 | **Nevada** | **Harry Reid** |
| 176 | | Nevada | Joe Heck |
| 177 | 21 | **New Hampshire** | **Kelly Ayotte** |
| 178 | | New Jersey | Frank Lautenberg |
| 179 | | New Jersey 1 | Rob Andrews |
| 180 | | New Jersey 2 | Frank LoBiondo |
| 181 | | New Jersey 4 | Chris H. Smith |
| 182 | | New Jersey 5 | Scott Garrett |
| 183 | | New Jersey 6 | Frank Pallone |
| 184 | | New Jersey 7 | Leonard Lance |
| 185 | | New Jersey 8 | Albio Sires |
| 186 | | New Jersey 9 | Bill Pascrel |
| 187 | | New Jersey 11 | Rodney Frelinghuysen |

187

| | | | | | | |
|---|---|---|---|---|---|---|
| 188 | **22** | **New York** | **Chuck Schumer** | 232 | **27** | **Oregon** | **Ron Wyden** |
| 189 | | New York 2 | Peter T. King | 233 | | Oregon 2 | Greg Walden |
| 190 | | New York 3 | Steve Israel | 234 | | Oregon 3 | Earl Blumenauer |
| 191 | | New York 5 | Gregory Meeks | 235 | | Oregon 4 | Peter DeFazio |
| 192 | | New York 7 | Nydia Velázquez | 236 | | Oregon 5 | Kurt Schrader |
| 193 | | New York 9 | Yvette Clarke | 237 | **28** | **Pennsylvania** | **Pat Toomey** |
| 194 | | New York 10 | Jerrold Nadler | 238 | | Pennsylvania 1 | Bob Brady |
| 195 | | New York 12 | Carolyn B. Maloney | 239 | | Pennsylvania 2 | Chaka Fattah |
| 196 | | New York 13 | Charles B. Rangel | 240 | | Pennsylvania 3 | Mike Kelly |
| 197 | | New York 14 | Joseph Crowley | 241 | | Pennsylvania 5 | Glenn Thompson |
| 198 | | New York 15 | José Serrano | 242 | | Pennsylvania 6 | Jim Gerlach |
| 199 | | New York 16 | Eliot Engel | 243 | | Pennsylvania 7 | Pat Meehan |
| 200 | | New York 17 | Nita Lowey | 244 | | Pennsylvania 8 | Mike Fizpatrick |
| 201 | | New York 19 | Chris Gibson | 245 | | Pennsylvania 9 | Bill Shuster |
| 202 | | New York 20 | Paul Tonko | 246 | | Pennsylvania 10 | Tom Marino |
| 203 | | New York 22 | Paul Tonko | 247 | | Pennsylvania 11 | Lou Barletta |
| 204 | | New York 23 | Tom Reed | 248 | | Pennsylvania 14 | Michael F. Doyle |
| 205 | | New York 25 | Louise Slaughter | 249 | | Pennsylvania 15 | Charlie Dent |
| 206 | | New York 26 | Brian Higgins | 250 | | Pennsylvania 16 | Joe Pitts |
| 207 | **23** | **North Carolina** | **Richard Burr** | 251 | | Pennsylvania 18 | Timothy F. Murphy |
| 208 | | North Carolina 1 | George K. Butterfield | 252 | | Rhode Island 1 | David Cicilline |
| 209 | | North Carolina 2 | Renee Ellmers | 253 | | Rhode Island 2 | James Langevin |
| 210 | | North Carolina 3 | Walter B. Jones | 254 | **29** | **South Carolina** | **Tim Scott** |
| 211 | | North Carolina 4 | David E. Price | 255 | | South Carolina | Lindsey Graham |
| 212 | | North Carolina 5 | Virginia Foxx | 256 | | South Carolina 2 | Joe Wilson |
| 213 | | North Carolina 10 | Patrick McHenry | 257 | | South Carolina 3 | Jeff Duncan |
| 214 | **24** | **North Dakota** | **John Hoeven** | 258 | | South Carolina 4 | Trey Gowdy |
| 215 | | New Jersey 9 | Bill Pascrell | 259 | | South Carolina 5 | Mick Mulvaney |
| 216 | | New Mexico | Tom Udall | 260 | | South Carolina 6 | Jim Clyburn |
| 217 | | New Mexico 3 | Ben R. Luján | 261 | **30** | **South Dakota** | **John Thune** |
| 218 | **25** | **Ohio** | **Rob Portman** | 262 | | South Dakota | Kristi Noem |
| 219 | | Ohio 4 | Jim Jordan | 263 | | Tennessee 1 | Phil Roe |
| 220 | | Ohio 5 | Bob Latta | 264 | | Tennessee 2 | Jimmy Duncan |
| 221 | | Ohio 6 | Bill Johnson | 265 | | Tennessee 3 | Chuck Fleischmann |
| 222 | | Ohio 7 | Bob Gibbs | 266 | | Tennessee 4 | Scott DesJarlais |
| 223 | | Ohio 9 | Marcy Kaptur | 267 | | Tennessee 5 | Jim Cooper |
| 224 | | Ohio 10 | Mike Turner | 268 | | Tennessee 6 | Diane Black |
| 225 | | Ohio 11 | Marcia Fudge | 269 | | Tennessee 7 | Marsha Blackburn |
| 226 | | Ohio 12 | Pat Tiberi | 270 | | Tennessee 8 | stephen Fincher |
| 227 | | Ohio 13 | Tim Ryan | 271 | | Tennessee 9 | Steve Cohen |
| 228 | | Ohio 15 | steve stivers | | | | |
| 229 | | Ohio 16 | Jim Renacci | | | | |
| 230 | **26** | **Oklahoma** | **James Lankford** | | | | |
| 231 | | Oklahoma 3 | Frank D. Lucas | | | | |

| | | | | | | |
|---|---|---|---|---|---|---|
| 272 | | Texas 1 | Louie Gohmert | 312 | **33** | **Washington** | **Patty Murray** |
| 273 | | Texas 2 | Ted Poe | 313 | | Washington 2 | Rick Larsen |
| 274 | | Texas 3 | Sam Johnson | 314 | | Washington 3 | J. Herrera Beutler |
| 275 | | Texas 5 | Jeb Hensarling | 315 | | Washington 5 | Cathy McMorris Rodgers |
| 276 | | Texas 6 | Joe Barton | 316 | | Washington 7 | Jim McDermott |
| 277 | | Texas 7 | John Culberson | 317 | | Washington 8 | Dave Reichert |
| 278 | | Texas 8 | Kevin Brady | 318 | | Washington 9 | Adam Smith |
| 279 | | Texas 9 | Al Green | 319 | | West Virginia 1 | David McKinley |
| 280 | | Texas 10 | Michael McCaul | 320 | **34** | **Wisconsin** | **Ron Johnson** |
| 281 | | Texas 11 | Mike Conaway | 321 | | Wisconsin 1 | Paul Ryan |
| 282 | | Texas 12 | Kay Granger | 322 | | Wisconsin 3 | Ron Kind |
| 283 | | Texas 13 | Mac Thornberry | 323 | | Wisconsin 4 | Gwen Moore |
| 284 | | Texas 15 | Rubén Hinojosa | 324 | | Wisconsin 5 | Jim Sensenbrenner |
| 285 | | Texas 17 | Bill Flores | 325 | | Wisconsin 7 | Sean Duffy |
| 286 | | Texas 18 | Sheila Jackson-Lee | 326 | | Wisconsin 8 | Reid Ribble |
| 287 | | Texas 19 | Randy Neugebauer | 327 | | Wyoming | Mike Enzi |
| 288 | | Texas 21 | Lamar S. Smith | 328 | | Wyoming | Cynthia Lummis |
| 289 | | Texas 22 | Pete Olson | 329 | | District of Columbia | Eleanor Norton |
| 290 | | Texas 24 | Kenny Marchant | 330 | | American Samoa | Amata Coleman |
| 291 | | Texas 26 | Michael C. Burgess | 331 | | Guam | Madeleine Bordallo |
| 292 | | Texas 27 | Blake Farenthold | 332 | | Islands | Gregorio Sablan |
| 293 | | Texas 28 | Henry Cuellar | 333 | | Pueto Rico | Pedro Rierluisis |
| 294 | | Texas 29 | Gene Green | 334 | | Virgin Islands | Stacey Plaskett |
| 295 | | Texas 30 | Eddie B. Johnson | | | | |
| 296 | | Texas 31 | John Carter | | | | |
| 297 | | Texas 32 | Pete Sessions | | | | |
| 298 | | Texas 35 | Lloyd Doggett | | | | |
| 299 | **31** | **Utah** | **Mike Lee** | | | | |
| 300 | | Utah 1 | Rob Bishop | | | | |
| 301 | | Utah 3 | Jason Chaffetz | | | | |
| 302 | **32** | **Vermont** | **Patrick Leahy** | | | | |
| 303 | | Virginia | Peter Welch | | | | |
| 304 | | Virginia 1 | Rob Wittman | | | | |
| 305 | | Virginia 2 | Scott Rigell | | | | |
| 306 | | Virginia 3 | Bobby Scott | | | | |
| 307 | | Virginia 4 | Randy Forbes | | | | |
| 308 | | Virginia 5 | Bob Goodlatte | | | | |
| 309 | | Virginia 6 | Bob Goodlatte | | | | |
| 310 | | Virginia 9 | Morgan Griffith | | | | |
| 311 | | Virginia 11 | Gerry Connolly | | | | |

189

The number in bold to the right of each name is the estimated time in office upon expiration of their class. The names in bold have been in office 12 to 42 years.

| State | Class I Expire 2018 | YRS | Class II Expire 2020 | YRS | Class III Expire 2016 | YRS |
|---|---|---|---|---|---|---|
| 1 Alabama | | | Jeff Sessions (R) | 24 | **Richard Shelby (R)** | 30 |
| 2 Alaska | | | Dan Sullivan (R) | 6 | **Lisa Murkowski (R)** | 14 |
| 3 Arizona | Jeff Flake (R) | 6 | | | **John McCain (R)** | 30 |
| 4 Arkansas | | | Tom Cotton (R) | 6 | John Boozman (R) | 6 |
| 5 California | **Dianne Feinstein (D)** | 24 | | | **Barbara Boxer (D)** | 24 |
| 6 Colorado | | | Cory Gardner (R) | 6 | **Michael Bennet (D)** | 8 |
| 7 Connecticut | Chris Murphy (D) | 6 | | | **Richard Blumenthal** | 12 |
| 8 Delaware | **Tom Carper (D)** | 18 | **Chris Coons (D)** | 12 | | |
| 9 Florida | **Bill Nelson (D)** | 18 | | | Marco Rubio (R) | 6 |
| 10 Georgia | | | David Perdue (R) | 6 | **Johnny Isakson (R)** | 12 |
| 11 Hawaii | Mazie Hirono (D) | 6 | | | Brian Schatz (D) | 4 |
| 12 Idaho | | | **Jim Risch (R)** | 12 | **Mike Crapo (R)** | 18 |
| 13 Illinois | | | **Dick Durbin (D)** | 24 | Mark Kirk (R) | 6 |
| 14 Indiana | Joe Donnelly (D) | 6 | | | Dan Coats (R) | 6 |
| 15 Iowa | | | Joni Ernst (R) | 6 | **Chuck Grassley (R)** | 36 |
| 16 Kansas | | | **Pat Roberts (R)** | 24 | Jerry Moran (R) | 6 |
| 17 Kentucky | | | **Mitch McConnell (R)** | 36 | Rand Paul (R) | 6 |
| 18 Louisiana | | | Bill Cassidy (R) | 6 | **David Vitter (R)** | 12 |
| 19 Maine | Angus King (I) | 6 | **Susan Collins (R)** | 24 | | |
| 20 Maryland | **Ben Cardin (D)** | 12 | | | **Barbara Mikulski (D)** | 30 |
| 21 Massachusetts | Elizabeth Warren (D) | 6 | Ed Markey (D) | 6 | | |
| 22 Michigan | **Debbie Stabenow (D)** | 18 | Gary Peters (D) | 6 | | |
| 23 Minnesota | **Amy Klobuchar (D)** | 12 | **Al Franken (D)** | 12 | | |
| 24 Mississippi | **Roger Wicker (R)** | 12 | **Thad Cochran (R)** | 42 | | |
| 25 Missouri | **Claire McCaskill (D)** | 12 | | | Roy Blunt (R) | 6 |
| 26 Montana | **Jon Tester (D)** | 12 | Steve Daines (R) | 6 | | |
| 27 Nebraska | Deb Fischer (R) | 6 | Ben Sasse (R) | 6 | | |
| 28 Nevada | Dean Heller (R) | 6 | | | **Harry Reid (D)** | 30 |
| 29 New Hampshire | | | **Jeanne Shaheen (D)** | 12 | Kelly Ayotte (R) | 6 |
| 30 New Jersey | **Bob Menendez (D)** | 12 | Cory Booker (D) | 6 | | |
| 31 New Mexico | Martin Heinrich (D) | 6 | **Tom Udall (D)** | 12 | | |
| 32 New York | **Kirsten Gillibrand (D)** | 10 | | | **Chuck Schumer (D)** | 18 |
| 33 North Carolina | | | Thom Tillis (R) | 6 | **Richard Burr (R)** | 12 |
| 34 North Dakota | Heidi Heitkamp (D) | 6 | | | John Hoeven (R) | 6 |
| 35 Ohio | **Sherrod Brown (D)** | 12 | | | Rob Portman (R) | 6 |
| 36 Oklahoma | | | Jim Inhofe (R) | 22 | James Lankford (R) | 6 |
| 37 Oregon | | | **Jeff Merkley (D)** | 12 | **Ron Wyden (D)** | 20 |
| 38 Pennsylvania | **Bob Casey, Jr. (D)** | 12 | | | Pat Toomey (R) | 6 |
| 39 Rhode Island | **Sheldon Whitehouse D** | 12 | **Jack Reed (D)** | 24 | | |
| 40 South Carolina | | | **Lindsey Graham (R)** | 18 | Tim Scott (R) | 6 |
| 41 South Dakota | | | Mike Rounds (R) | 6 | **John Thune (R)** | 12 |
| 42 Tennessee | **Bob Corker (R)** | 12 | **Lamar Alexander (R)** | 18 | | |
| 43 Texas | Ted Cruz (R) | 6 | **John Cornyn (R)** | 18 | | |
| 44 Utah | **Orrin Hatch (R)** | 40 | | | Mike Lee (R) | |
| 45 Vermont | **Bernie Sanders (I)** | 12 | | | **Patrick Leahy (D)** | 42 |
| 46 Virginia | Tim Kaine (D) | 6 | **Mark Warner (D)** | 12 | | |
| 47 Washington | **Maria Cantwell (D)** | 18 | | | **Patty Murray (D)** | 24 |
| 48 West Virginia | Joe Manchin (D) | 6 | Shelley Moore Capito | 6 | | |
| 49 Wisconsin | Tammy Baldwin (D) | 6 | | | Ron Johnson (R) | 6 |
| 50 Wyoming | **John Barrasso (R)** | 12 | **Mike Enzi (R)** | 24 | | |

TOTAL = 100      33 - Class I Senators      33 - Class II Senators      34 - Class III Senators

190

## About the Author

Howard Hanson is a problem solving individual that is enthusiastic, energetic and an effective communicator. He has been a businessman, ME, CBR, Franchisor, inventor, patent writer, patent holder, software designer, web designer, public speaker, sales trainer, 2nd Degree Black Belt and a medical and political advocate.

At the age of 24, Howard was already managing the largest electrical automation, motor control, and fire alarm project in his state. He has worked with FERC's **F**ederal **E**nergy **R**egulatory **C**ommissioner rebuilding a Levee. Additionally, Howard founded a business that saved 10's of millions of dollars in energy a year, a number one supplier in the U.S., and sat on the board of directors of the Wisconsin Public Service Commission (PSC) and chaired two sub-committees alongside the vice presidents of electric utility companies. Howard has wide support in the form of letters from Congressmen and the executive branch for an energy program that he has developed as an alternative in the U.S., the details of which he will publish in his upcoming book, "Making America Energy Independent." Howard's desire to make things better has lead him to start writing books - and what better place to start then at the top? A book on electing our leaders! Email me at: howard@howtoreplacecongress.com

# Reference List

1. Herbst, Jurgen. "The Once and Future School: Three Hundred and Fifty Years of American Secondary Education." New York: Routledge, 1996

2. "List of American Federal Politicians Convicted of Crimes." *Wikipedia*. Wikimedia Foundation, n.d. Web. 10 Oct. 2016.

3. "Senate Historical Office." *U.S. Senate: The Senate and the United States Constitution*. United States Senate, n.d. Web. 10 Oct. 2016.

4. "Congressional Voting Turnout Is at Lowest Mark Since 1978." *News Releases*. The United States Census Bureau, 16 July 2015. Web. 19 Sept. 2016.

5. Hamilton, Alexander, James Madison, and John Jay. "Federalist No. 60." *The Federalist Papers* (2009): 153-56. Web. 6 Oct. 2016.

6. Classroom, By Annenberg. "Amendment XVII Popular Election of Senators."*National Constitution Center*. N.p., n.d. Web. 06 Oct. 2016.

7. "More than Two Dozen Members of Congress Have Been Indicted since 1980."*The Fix*. The Washington Post, n.d. Web. 07 Oct. 2016.

8. Washington, George. "Washington's Farewell Address 1796."*Lillian Goldman Law Library*. Yale Law School, 2008. Web. 10 Oct. 2016.

9. Story, Joseph. *Commentaries on the Constitution of the United States*. 2 volumes, fifth edition. Edited by Melville Bigelow. Boston: Little, Brown, and Company, 1891.

10. McCutcheon v. Fed. Election Comm'n 572 U.S. 572 12-536. US Supreme Court. 2 Apr. 2014. *Justia Law*. Justia, 2014`. Web. 10 Oct. 2016.

11. Edsall, Thomas B. "Anger Can Be Power - Opinionator - The New York Times."*The Opinion Pages*. The New York Times, 8 Oct. 2013. Web. 7 Oct. 2016.

12. Edsall, Thomas B. "The Shadow Lobbyist - Opinionator - The New York Times."*The Opinion Pages*. The New York Times, 25 Apr. 2013. Web. 7 Oct. 2016.

13. Dilanian, Ken. "Lobbyists Find More Ways to Bond with Lawmakers." *USA Today*. Gannett, 31 Jan. 2008. Web. 07 Oct. 2016.

14. Ro, Sam. "This is the Best Ilustration of History's Bull and Bear Markets We've Seen Yet." *Business Insider.* 31 Dec 2014. 3 Oct. 2016.

15. Jones, Jeffrey. "Ahead of Midterms, Anti-Incumbent Sentiment Strong in U.S." Gallup. May 14, 2014. Web. 27 Oct. 2014.

16. Hirano, Shigeo, and James M. Snyder. "Primary Elections and Political Accountability: What Happens to Incumbents in Scandals?" Harvard University. Columbia University. 2012. Web. 16 Oct. 2014.

17. Friedman, John, and Richard Holdman. "The Rising Incumbent Reelection Rate: What is Gerrymandering Got to Do With It?' Harvard University. 29 May 2008. Web. 16 Oct. 2014.

18. Cali, Jeanine. "Frequent Reference Question: How Many Federal Laws Are There?" *Library of Congress Blogs*. Library of Congress, 12 Mar. 2013. Web. 24 Feb. 2016.

19. Koempel, Michael L., Judy Schneider, and Christina Wu. "The First Day of a New Congress: A Guide to Proceedings on the Senate Floor." 26 Feb. 2014. Web. 15 Oct. 2014

20. "Charters of Freedom." *U.S. Senate: Constitution of the United States.* United States Senate, 1994. Web. 14 Oct. 2014

21. "Cost of the Future Newly Insured under the Affordable Care Act (ACA)." Society of Actuaries. 1 Mar. 2013. Web. 15 Oct. 2014

22. "New FBI Data Shows Mental Health Records in Background Check System Tripled Since Release of Fatal Gaps Report Pressed States to Submit Records of Prohibited Gun Purchasers." *Everytown for Gun Safety - Press*. Everytown for Gun Safety, 22 May 2014. Web. 10 Oct. 2016.

23. Savio Joe. "PBS Nova Rise of the Drones". Online Video Clip. Youtube. Youtube, 12 Feb. 2013. Web. 15 Jul 2016.

24. Preston, Julia. "Number of Illegal Immigrants in U.S. May Be on Rise Again, Estimates Say." *The New York Times*. The New York Times, 23 Sept. 2013. Web. 27 Oct. 2014.

25. Runningen, Roger, and Jeff Kearns. "Obama Angers Latino Allies by Delaying Immigration Change." Bloomberg Business Week, 6 Sept. 2014. Web. 15 Oct. 2014.

26. Obama, Barack. "Remarks by President Obama in Address to the United Nations General Assembly." Speech, United Nations, New York, NY, 24 Sept, 2013. N.d.

27. McDonald, Michael P. "Voter Turnout in the 2010 Midterm Election." The Forum 8, no. 4 (2010).

28. Selyukh, Alina. "FCC Proposal Would Limit What Internet Providers Coan Do With Users' Data>" *NPR WLRN.* 10 Mar 2016. Web. 3 Oct. 2016

29. "Glossary - Class." *United States Senate - Reference.* United States Senate, 1994. Web. 1 Oct. 2016.

30. "1787: Senators Receive Class Assignments-- May 15, 1789." *Senate Historical Office.* United States Senate, 1994. Web. 10 Oct. 2016.

31. Dinan, Stephen. "Supreme Court Rules in Redistricting Case: Illegal Immigrants Can Be Counted." *Washington Times.* The Washington Times, 4 Apr. 2016. Web. 1 Oct. 2016.

32. Kellett, Jenny. "Do You Need a Passport to Travel in Europe?" *USA Today.* Gannett, n.d. Web. 10 Oct. 2016.

33. FairUS. "The Fiscal Burden of Illegal Immigration on United States Taxpayers (2013)." *Federation for American Immigration Reform.* FairUS.org, July 2010. Web. 10 Oct. 2016.

34. Querubin, P. "Political reform and elite persistence: Term limits and political dynasties in the Philippines." *Mimeo.* Massachusetts Institute of Technology. 2011 Web. 12 Jan. 2016.

35. Dobbs, Lou. "Lobbying Against America." *CNNMoney*. Cable News Network, 11 Aug. 2005. Web. 16 Oct. 2014.

36. Rosiak, Luke. "Frequent Frankers in Congress Face Tough Re-election Fights."*Washington Examiner*. The Washington Examiner, 27 Aug. 2014. Web. 16 Oct. 2014.

37. Brown, Lyle C et al. "The Politics of Interest Groups." In Practicing Texas Politics. 2011-2012 ed. Boston, MA: Suzanne Jeans, 2012.

38. Peterson, Kristina. "Paul Ryan Unveils GOP Plan to Balance Budget in 10 Years." *WSJ*. Wsj.com, 01 Apr. 2014. Web. 3 Oct. 2016.

39. "Senate Historical Office." *U.S. Senate: The Senate and the United States Constitution*. United States Senate, 1994. Web. 10 Oct. 2016.

40. "First Family Vacations - Judicial Watch." *Judicial Watch*. Judicial Watch, Inc., 2014. Web. 29 Oct. 2014.

41. Taylor, Steven. "Madison's Definitions of Republic." *Outside the Beltway*. 5 Jun. 2011. 17 Oct. 2014

42. Mader, Dave, Steven Kelman, and Jeff Myers. "What It Takes to Change Government." *Booz Allan Hamilton*. Booz Allan Ham lton, n.d. Web. 10 Oct. 2016.

43. "What Is Centrist/Centrism." *The Centrist Party*. N.p., n.d. Web. 16 Oct. 2014.

44. Nakamura, David, and Debbi Wilgoren. "Caught on Open Mike, Obama Tells Medvedev He Needs 'space' on Missile Defense." *Washington Post - Politics*. The Washington Post, 26 Mar. 2012. Web. 10 Oct. 2016.

45. Kessler, Glenn. "Harry Reid's Claim That Congress Rates Lower than North Korea." *Washington Post*. The Washington Post, 15 Jul. 2013. Web. 16 Oct. 2014.

46. Jan, Tracy. "For Freshmen in Congress, Focus Is on Raising Money." *The Boston Globe*. The Boston Globe, 12 May 2013. Web. 16 Oct. 2014.

47. Grimm, Ryan. "Call Time For Congress Shows How Fundrais ng

Dominates Bleak Work Life." *The Huffington Post.* The Huffington Post, 8 Jan. 2013. Web. 16 Oct. 2014.

48. Lipman-Blumen, Jean. "The Allure of Toxic Leaders." *The Economist.* The Economist, 2004. Web. 3 Oct. 2016.

49. "More than Two Dozen Members of Congress Have Been Indicted since 1980."*The Fix.* The Washington Post, n.d. Web. 07 Oct. 2016.

50. "Barack Obama Executive Orders Subjects." *Federal Register.* National Archives and Records Administration, 2009. Web. 11 Oct. 2016.

51. "U.S. Propane Residential Price". *Petroleum & Other Liquids.* U.S. Energy Information Administration. 1992-2016. Web. 10 Oct 2016.

52. Muy, Ylan Q. "Americans Saw Wealth Plummet 40 Percent from 2007 to 2010, Federal Reserve Says." The Washington Post, 11 Jun. 2012. Web. 20 Oct. 2014.

53. Coles, Dave. "Verizon, NSA Spying and the Threat to Canadians' Privacy and National Security." Rabble.ca. 20 Aug. 2013. Web. 17 Oct. 2014.

54. Selyukh, Alina. "FCC Proposal Would Limit What Internet Providers Coan Do With Users' Data>" *NPR WLRN.* 10 Mar 2016. Web. 3 Oct 2016.

55. Vlahos, Kelley Beaucar. "Scrap Heap Of War: Billions In Equipment Being Left Behind In Afghanistan." *Fox News Politics.* FOX News Network, 04 Apr. 2014. Web. 07 Oct. 2016.

56. Klaymann, Larry (10 June 2013). "Verizon Complaint aka Klaymann et al v. Obama et al in Civil Action No.: 1:13-cv-00851 in the United States District Court for the District of Columbia". Freedom Watch. Web.16 Oct 2014.

57. News, ABC. "Verizon Sells Landlines in 14 States to Frontier in $8.6B Deal."*ABC News.* ABC News Network, n.d. Web. 11 Oct. 2016.

58. Setoodeh, Ramin. "Sylvester Stallone on Donald Trump, Republicans and Running for Office." *Yahoo! Movies.* Yahoo!, 8 Jan. 2016. Web. 11 Oct. 2016

www.ingramcontent.com/pod-product-compliance
Lightning Source LLC
Chambersburg PA
CBHW060254290526
45789CB00001B/320